Deliciously Kosher

Traditional and Contemporary Recipes • Valley Beth Shalom Sisterhood

Deliciously Kosher

Traditional and Contemporary Recipes • Valley Beth Shalom Sisterhood

ISBN 978-1-62620-866-7

Acknowledgements

The heart and soul of a Jewish home has been traditionally represented in food. This cookbook is the result of the collaborative effort from the Sisterhood of Valley Beth Shalom Synagogue in Encino, California. Our hope is that these recipes will bring the joy of good food to your home just as they have done to ours. We share with you both traditional and contemporary recipes that can be enjoyed on Shabbat, holidays and every day of the year.

Our many thanks are extended to all who have contributed as chefs, writers, and proofreaders. Their energy and dedication has culminated in the creation of this cookbook. Our heartfelt thanks and gratitude are given to Jennifer Rea Hardin, Michelle Spiegel and Barbara Gales-Miller — without their vision and hard work, this cookbook would have remained a dream. A special thank you to Joyce Goldman, our 'proofreader extraordinaire', who worked overtime helping prepare the book for the publisher. A very special thank you to Alice Gordezky, our graphic designer, who got us to the finish line. Above all we extend our thanks to you and your families for bringing our cookbook into your home and demonstrating your support of Valley Beth Shalom Sisterhood. We wish you and your family happiness, love and a lot of good cooking, through ***Deliciously Kosher***.

Thank You

Thank you to all the talented cooks, testers, writers and proofreaders who went above and beyond by donating their time, energy and recipes to the building of this cookbook. We received more than 1,000 recipes from the members, families and friends of Valley Beth Shalom. Regretfully, due to space limitations and duplications, we were unable to include every submitted recipe. We hope that we have not inadvertently omitted any contributors.

Christy Abramovitch
Tahli Abramovitch
Jean Adatto
Charlotte Adelman
Debbie Alden
Rob Anker
Cecile Appel
Ricki Averbach
Zane Averbach
Kelleen Balle
Pearl Barocas
Bernice Baron
Evelyn Bauer
Paige Beck
Annette Beezy
Phyllis Beim
Shirley Bekas
Susan Bender
Nancy Berger
Bella Bergman
Shanna Berkovits
Sylvia Berle
Ilene Berman
Ruth Binder
Heather Binder
Gail Black
Carolyn Block
Sandy Bollinger
Tiffany Boxer
Zella Brainen
Susan Brender
Susan Broder
Sharon Bronte
Renee Brownstein
Ellen Brownstein
Irene Burstein
Jeri Cohen
Sandra Cohen
Annette Cohen
Linda Cole-Barlam
Pearl Cutler
Nanette Cutler
Dianna Davidson
Deborah Davis
Linda Dennis
Janet Djalilmand
Jill Donaty
Tina Donay
Joel Douglas
Amee Faggen
Eda Faierman
Justin Field
Tessa Finder
Adinah Finn
Marjorie Forman
Cindy Franklin
Rose Freed
Wendy Freed
Lori Freson
Joyce Fried
Arlene Friedman
Dorothy Friss
Karen Fryman
Barbara Gales-Miller
Judy Geller-Wollstein
Gloria Getzug

Terri Getzug
Elaine Gill
Ruth Ginsberg
Zita Gluskin
Evelyn Golan
Bella Goldberg
Francine Golden
Marilyn Golden
Alyse Golden-Berkley
Jessica Goldklang
Joyce Goldman
Danielle Goldsmith
Robin Greene
Alice Greenfield
Ethel Greenstein
Roslyn Grinberg
Barrie Grobstein
Amy Gross
Sharon Grossman
Cynthia Hamburg
Corine Hartman
Sharon Hasson
Lisa Hestrin-Lerner
Darlene Hirschinger
Becky Hoffman
Angela Horvitz
Marlene Horwitz
Marcie Howard
Jim Howland
Judy Jackson
Patti Jacobs
Cheree Kahn
Tobey Kaplan
Eudice Kaplan
Jo Ann Kapper
Shelly Karpman
Carol Kaufman
Beverly Keyser
Gail King
Debbie Kloman
Betty Kout
Sharon Krischer
Roz Krojansky
Helaine Kroll
Linda Kulber
Sandra Kussin
Monica Lacher
Karen Landman
Phyllis Lapin
Sandy Leib
Charlotte Leib
Barbara Leimberg
Phyllis Lemberger
Allyn Levine
Emily Levine
Lila Levy
Lillian Liebross
Rita Lipshutz
Helen Longwill
Rhea Lorberg
Bobby Lowenkron
Loretta Lowenstein
Shirley Lowy
Ronda Machlovitz
Kelleen McCormack
Clenn Melnick
Kait Miller
Rush Miller
Myra Miller
Marla Milner
Grace Mitnick
Sandy Mittleman
Monica Mohilef
Anna Moraiy
Jill Morganstein
Barbara Mortimer
Merideth Mounce
Debbie Muer
Robin Muer
Dorothy Naftalin
Debbie Nelson
Carol Neumark
Bunny North
Susan North-Gilboa
Jo-Anne Novik
Maya Nozar
Jacob Olinka

Juliana Olinka
Sheila Paley
Toni Parker
Debbie Pearlman
Robin Permaul
Evelyn Pierson
Louise Pinsky
Julie Polkes
Debbie Posner
Mara Pressman
Lola Rabow
Wendy Racine
Orit Rappaport
Jennifer Rea Hardin
Jessica Reese-Wilner
Ariella Reisner
Mira Ress
Kathy Reuben
Susan Richter
David Rips
Noelle Rips
Gavi Roisman
Sharoni Ron
Harriet Rosenberg
Lori Rosenberg
Tobie Rosenberg
Linda Rosenblatt
Andrea Rosenwein
Carol Rosner
Harriet Rosvinsky
Larry Rush
Patti Said
Esther Saltzman
Sara Scharff
Violet Schlesinger
Karen Schwartzman
Colette Segal
Adele Selman-Strozer
Amy Shamash
Annette Shapiro
Laureen Shefman
Dalit Shtevy
Jan Shulman
Fran Shuster
Gail Silverstein
Judi Simon
Geri Sisko
Denise Smickler-Geller
Anne Smiler
Carol Solomon
Reba Soroky
Jackie Sosenblaum
Michelle Spiegel
Laurie Starre
Ilona Stein
Hilary Steinberg
Becky Stell
Beverly Sterman
Susan Tabibian
Sharon Thompson-Glass
Susan Tipton
Nancy Ugoretz
Stephanie Walsh
Jackie Waterman
Muriel Waterman
Sally Weber
Carla Weingarten
Phyllis Weinstein-Siebold
Stacey Weiss
Linda Weiss
Rita Wenger
Faye Wernick
Jennifer Wexler
Sally White
Claire Wilen
Lisa Wilen
Ms. Winnick
Taube Wiseman
Arlene Wolff
Arlene Zicklin
Elana Zimmerman
Vicki Zipperstein
Karolin Zoghi

Special Thanks to:
Rabbi Joshua Hoffman
Rabbi Noah Farkas

Table of Contents

Deliciously Kosher

Traditional and Contemporary Recipes • Valley Beth Shalom Sisterhood

Appetizers

Appetizers

Grandma Irene's Chopped Liver

2 medium to large onions
1/3 cup Schmaltz (chicken fat)
1 pound chicken livers
6 large or extra large eggs, hard-boiled
1 small to medium onion, chopped finely
salt and pepper, to taste

Chop 2 medium to large onions and fry in chicken fat until browned. Add chicken livers and fry until cooked. Do not overcook. Finely chop cooked livers and onions. Chop hard-boiled eggs and add to small to medium raw onion. Add salt and pepper to taste. Add chopped livers, onions and pan juice to egg/raw onion mixture. Stir until all ingredients are combined, adding salt and pepper to taste. Refrigerate overnight.

Chopped Liver

1 onion, diced
oil
paprika
1/2 pound chicken livers
4 hard-boiled eggs
1 tablespoon mayonnaise salad dressing
salt and pepper, to taste

Sauté onion in oil. Add a few sprinkles of paprika for color. Set onion aside. Add chicken liver and fry until done. Put cooked liver and hard-boiled eggs through a food grinder (not a food processor). Mix ground liver and eggs with onion and mayonnaise salad dressing. Add salt and pepper to taste. Serve with rye bread or crackers.

Vegetable Pâté – Mock Chopped Liver

1 garlic clove, minced
1 onion, sliced
8 ounces mushrooms
olive oil
1 cup walnuts, toasted lightly
5 hard-boiled eggs (whites only), chopped
salt, to taste

Sauté garlic, onion and mushrooms in olive oil. With food processor, chop walnuts. Add sautéed vegetables, eggs and salt. Can be frozen.

PITA CHIPS

2 6 inch pita pockets
nonstick cooking spray

Cut pita into eighths, split each triangle in half along outside seam. Then place rough side up on cookie sheet. Spray triangles with cooking spray. Bake 6 to 8 minutes, until crisp. Watch carefully, as they brown quickly.

Mock Chopped Liver

1 onion, chopped
olive oil
3 hard-boiled eggs, divided
3/4 cup finely chopped walnuts
1 15 ounce can sweet peas, well-drained
salt and pepper

Sauté onion in oil until soft and light brown. Put 2 eggs and all other ingredients into food processor. Mix; add salt and pepper, to taste. Place in serving bowl; grate third egg on top.

Gorgonzola Canapés

6 ounces Gorgonzola, crumbled
1/4 pound butter, softened
1/2 teaspoon celery salt
1/3 cup finely chopped pecans
rye bread toasted on 1 side and cut into 4 dozen cut-outs
paprika

Combine cheese, butter, celery salt and pecans. Spread mixture on untoasted side of bread. Sprinkle with paprika and broil until bubbly.

Cheese Fondue

1/2 pound Swiss cheese, shredded
1/2 pound Gruyère cheese, shredded
2 tablespoons cornstarch
1 garlic clove, peeled
1 cup dry white wine
1 tablespoon lemon juice
1 tablespoon Sherry Brandy, such as Kirsch
1 tablespoon Dijon mustard
1 pinch nutmeg

In a small bowl, coat cheese with cornstarch and set aside. Rub inside of pot with garlic. Over medium heat, add wine to lemon juice and bring to simmer. Gradually stir cheese into liquid. Melt gradually. Once smooth, stir in brandy, mustard and nutmeg. Suggestions for dipping: Granny Smith apples, bread, broccoli, carrots.

Caramelized Onion and Sour Cream Spread

2 tablespoons plus 1/3 cup olive oil
1 large red onion, thinly sliced
1 large red bell pepper, thinly sliced
1/2 fennel bulb, cored, thinly sliced
2 teaspoons Herbes de Provence
1 teaspoon sugar
9 garlic cloves, finely chopped
1/3 cup sour cream
salt and pepper
sliced olive or French bread

Heat 2 tablespoons olive oil in heavy large skillet over medium heat. Add onion and next 4 ingredients. Cover; cook until vegetables release their juices, stirring occasionally, about 12 minutes. Uncover; sauté until juices evaporate, about 10 minutes. Add garlic; cook until vegetables are very tender and just beginning to brown, about 12 minutes longer. Cool completely. Purée vegetable mixture and sour cream in processor until almost smooth. Season spread generously with salt and pepper. Transfer to bowl. Preheat broiler. Arrange bread slices on baking sheet. Brush both sides of bread slices with 1/3 cup oil. Broil until golden, about 2 minutes per side. Cool. Serve with spread.

Dried Fruit Cheese Spread

Yield: Serves 10
Prep Time: 5 Minutes
Cooking Time: 3-5 Minutes

1/2 cup dark or light corn syrup
1/8 teaspoon salt
1/2 cup mixed dried fruit (such as raisins, dates, cherries, cranberries, currants, chopped apricots)
1/4 cup slivered almonds
3/4 teaspoon crushed red pepper
1/2 teaspoon almond extract
1 8 ounce package cream cheese
crackers

Mix corn syrup, salt, dried fruit, almonds, crushed pepper and almond extract in a saucepan. Heat to simmer, while stirring to blend. Remove from heat and let cool for 10 minutes. Place cream cheese on a platter. Top with fruit mixture. Serve with crackers. Can use Brie instead of cream cheese.

Salmon Ball

1 can red sockeye salmon, bones and skin removed
1 8 ounce package cream cheese
1 tablespoon lemon juice
1 tablespoon instant minced onion
2 to 3 tablespoons horseradish, drained
1/2 teaspoon salt
1/2 teaspoon Worcestershire sauce
pecans, chopped, optional

Combine salmon and cream cheese. Mix in lemon juice, onion, 2 tablespoons horseradish, salt and Worcestershire sauce. Taste; add more horseradish, if desired. Refrigerate until firm; roll into a ball. Roll in chopped pecans (optional). Can be made a day ahead. Serve with crackers.

Smoked Salmon Cheesecake

Yield: Serves 10-12 as an appetizer

1 1/2 pounds cream cheese, softened to room temperature
4 large eggs
1/4 cup half-and-half
1/2 cup minced onion
2 teaspoons butter or margarine
1/4 cup fresh chopped dill or 1/8 cup dried dill weed
4 ounces grated Swiss cheese
8 ounces smoked Nova salmon

Preheat oven to 300 degrees. With a mixer, cream together cream cheese, eggs and half-and-half. Sauté onions in butter or margarine. Add sautéed onions, dill, Swiss cheese and salmon; mix to blend all ingredients together. Pour mixture into a greased 9-inch springform pan. Wrap outside bottom and sides well with aluminum foil to prevent any leaks or water seeping in. Place filled springform pan in a water bath (another pan that it will fit into with boiling water coming at least half way up sides of springform pan). Bake at 300 degrees for 45 minutes, then turn off oven and let cheesecake cool in oven. Remove from oven when cool, cover and refrigerate or freeze. Can be served warm, at room temperature, or cold, depending on whether you want to spread it on bagels, breads, crackers, etc. Cut it in slices and serve like a piece of cake.

Herring Supreme

Yield: Serves 12

1 jar wine herring, drained, cut into pieces
1 jar chili sauce
1 green pepper, thinly sliced
1 tomato, thinly sliced
1/2 onion, thinly sliced
1 tablespoon vinegar

Mix together and marinate 1 to 2 days in refrigerator, before serving.

Hot Dog Hors d'Oeuvres

Yield: Serves 10

1 pound hot dogs, cut in small pieces or cocktail franks
3/4 cup bourbon or rye whiskey
1/2 cup ketchup
1/2 cup brown sugar
1 tablespoon grated onion

Put all ingredients in saucepan. Simmer for 1 hour. If liquid dries up, add more bourbon or rye whiskey. Place in casserole dish and serve.

Salami Hors d'Oeuvres

Yield: Serves 15-20

1 large whole salami
1/2 to 3/4 jar apricot sauce or jelly
3 to 4 tablespoons Dijon mustard

Place whole salami on large sheet of foil. Score salami with X's. Mix apricot sauce or jelly with mustard and spread on salami. Seal foil tightly. Bake at 350 degrees for 2 1/2 to 3 hours, basting often. Slice and serve.

Can be barbecued, which makes it crispy.

Thanksgiving Leftover Turkey Casserole Dip

leftover stuffing
cranberry sauce
turkey, chopped or diced
gravy
top with mashed potatoes

Layer all ingredients in an ovenproof baking dish. Bake until potatoes are golden. Spread on pieces of bread as a dip.

Hummus

Yield: Makes 5 cups

2 cans garbanzo beans
2 tablespoons tahini
juice of 1 lemon to taste
1/4 cup parsley
1 teaspoon salt
1/2 teaspoon cumin
1/2 cup olive oil

Blend all ingredients in food processor until smooth and creamy. Serve with vegetables or pita chips.

PITA CHIPS

6 pita bread pockets
olive oil
kosher salt
Parmesan cheese
garlic powder, optional

Open pita into two halves. Cut pita bread in triangles. Brush with olive oil; sprinkle with kosher salt or Parmesan cheese. Bake at 400 degrees for 11 minutes, or until crisp.

Chickpeas with Cumin

2 cans chickpeas
3 tablespoons chopped flat-leaf parsley
1 small red onion, finely chopped
1 to 2 cloves garlic, finely chopped
1/4 cup lemon juice
2 tablespoons olive oil
2 teaspoons ground cumin

Drain and rinse chickpeas. Combine all ingredients in a large bowl and toss well.

Artichoke Spinach Hot Dip

Yield: Serves 10-15

2 cans artichoke hearts
1 10 ounce package chopped spinach
1/2 cup mayonnaise
1/2 cup sour cream
1 cup grated Parmesan cheese
1 pound pepper jack cheese, shredded

Drain artichokes and place in food processor, pulse until chunks are made. Place in a bowl. Place spinach into microwave and cook on high for 5 minutes. Squeeze spinach dry and add to artichokes. Mix in mayonnaise, sour cream and Parmesan cheese. Mix well and place into baking dish. Bake in 350 degree oven for 30 minutes. Remove from oven and top with pepper jack cheese. When cheese is melted, serve with bagel chips or bread sticks

Variation: Instead of spinach, add one can diced green chilies. Can also add one red onion, diced.

Spinach Balls & Sauce

Yield: Makes 50-75 balls

SPINACH BALLS
2 10 ounce packages frozen, chopped spinach, thawed and squeezed dry
2 cups herb stuffing mix, crushed
3 eggs
1/4 teaspoon nutmeg
5 ounce wedge of Parmesan cheese or 1 cup firmly packed, grated Parmesan
1 stick margarine, melted
4 green onions, finely chopped

Combine and mix well. Shape into 1-inch balls. Refrigerate until ready to bake. Bake at 350 degrees for 10 to 15 minutes, or until golden brown, on an ungreased baking sheet.

SAUCE
1/2 cup dry mustard
1/2 cup white vinegar
1/4 cup sugar
1 egg yolk

Combine mustard and vinegar; let sit for 4 hours. Mix sugar and egg yolk in a small pan. Add mustard and vinegar; heat. Stir constantly until sauce is slightly thickened. Serve with spinach balls.

Tasty Mexican Spinach Dip

1 onion, chopped
1 tablespoon oil
1 4 ounce can green chilies
1 14 ounce can diced plum tomatoes, drained
1 10 ounce package chopped spinach, thawed and drained
8 ounces cream cheese, room temperature, cut into chunks
10 to 12 ounces grated Monterey Jack cheese
1 cup half-and-half
1 tablespoon red wine vinegar
salt and pepper to taste
1 teaspoon minced garlic, optional
tortilla chips

Sauté onions in oil in a skillet over medium-heat until they are soft (about 4 minutes). Add green chilies and tomatoes; cook for 2 minutes more. Transfer to a bowl; stir in spinach, cream cheese, Monterey Jack cheese, half-and-half and vinegar. Season with salt, pepper and garlic (optional). Spoon mixture into a shallow baking dish or pie plate. Bake at 400 degrees for 35 minutes, until dip is bubbly and top is light brown. Serve with tortilla chips.

Note: This is a winner dip! Also, it can be made a day before serving. Just refrigerate the dip instead of baking it. Before baking the next day, bring the dip to room temperature.

Oven-Dried Tomatoes on Crostini

24 small tomatoes
2 heads garlic, each clove unpeeled but smashed with the side of a sharp knife
salt and freshly ground black pepper, to taste
3 tablespoons sugar
16 sprigs fresh thyme, with stems
3/4 cup olive oil
French baguette

Preheat oven to 300 degrees. Using a sharp knife, cut a shallow X in the skin at bottom of each tomato. Drop tomatoes, 2 or 3 at a time, into boiling water; count to 10 and then lift out with a slotted spoon and plunge into a bowl filled with ice and water. Peel tomatoes, cut in half and gently squeeze juice and seeds out of each half. Place tomato halves side by side, cut side down, on a well-oiled jelly-roll pan (baking sheet with sides). Scatter with garlic cloves; sprinkle with salt, pepper, sugar, thyme and olive oil. Bake for 3 to 4 hours, shaking pan occasionally so tomatoes do not stick, until all liquid in tomatoes has evaporated. Tomatoes will become very brown around edges. Immediately transfer with a spatula to a glass dish to cool in a single layer. Cover with plastic wrap and refrigerate. If keeping for more than 2 to 3 hours, cover with olive oil.

CROSTINI (TOASTED FRENCH BAGUETTE)
Slice a French baguette into 1/4 inch slices, brush with a thin coat of olive oil on both sides, toast for a few minutes in a 350 degree oven and turn bread; continue toasting for a few more minutes on other side.

Hot Cranberry Pecan and Blue Cheese Dip

Yield: Serves 8

1 cup whole-berry cranberry sauce
1/2 cup mayonnaise
1 cup crumbled blue cheese (about 4 ounces)
1/2 cup finely chopped pecans, toasted

Preheat oven to 350 degrees. In medium bowl, combine all ingredients. Spoon mixture into 3-cup casserole. Bake for 20 minutes or until golden. Serve with assorted crackers or vegetable dippers.

Fresh Southwestern Salsa

1 15 ounce can black beans, drained and rinsed
1 1/2 cups cooked corn
2 medium tomatoes, cut up
1 red pepper, cut up
1 green pepper, cut up
1/2 cup red onion, chopped
1 to 2 jalapeños, cut up
1/3 cup lime juice
1/3 cup olive oil
1/2 teaspoon cumin
1/3 cup cilantro
1/2 teaspoon cayenne pepper

Mix together and enjoy. Serve with tortilla chips or as a side salad.

Mexican Hot Dip

Yield: Serves 20

2 cups sour cream
2 8 ounce packages regular cream cheese, room temperature
2 cups (8 ounces) shredded four-cheese Mexican blend
1 package taco seasoning mix
1 4.5 ounce can black olives, drained
1 14.5 ounce can diced tomatoes, drained
1 4 ounce can green chilies, drained
tortilla chips

Beat sour cream, cream cheese and Mexican cheese blend in medium bowl with electric mixer, until well combined. Add next 4 ingredients; stir. Pour into 2-quart baking dish that has been sprayed with cooking spray. Can be frozen before baking. Bake in 325 degree oven for 50 minutes. Serve with tortilla chips.

Picadillo

2 pounds lean ground beef
1 pint jar green olives, drained
3 1.5 ounce boxes raisins or 1/2 box golden raisins
1 10 ounce can tomatoes and green chilies
2 4 .5 ounce cans chopped black olives
1 7 ounce can green chilies, chopped
2 small jars cocktail onions, including juice
1 15 ounce can sliced new potatoes, including liquid
1 bag slivered almonds
1 jar capers
1 1.25 ounce package taco seasoning mix
garlic powder, to taste

Brown beef. Chop or slice green olives into medium-sized pieces. Soak raisins in hot water for 10 minutes. Drain raisins. Add olives, raisins and remaining ingredients to beef. Simmer 10 minutes. Serve with pita or tortilla chips.

Variation: Replace capers with 1/2 box frozen peas.

Lox Mousse

1 pound cream cheese
3 to 6 ounces lox
2 tablespoons minced onion
2 tablespoons lemon juice

Beat cream cheese in mixer. Add lox; mix until blended. Add minced onion and lemon juice; blend well. Use as spread on bagels, crackers, pumpernickel or other bread.

Mango Quesadillas

Yield: Serves 4
Prep Time: 10 minutes

1 15 ounce can black beans, rinsed and drained (1 1/2 cups)
3 ounces goat cheese, crumbled (1/2 cup)
1 medium tomato, seeded and coarsely chopped
3/4 cup corn kernels (from 2 ears of corn)
1 large mango, peeled, pitted and chopped
1 small red onion, coarsely chopped
1/3 cup fresh cilantro, chopped
1 tablespoon plus 1 1/2 teaspoons coarsely chopped fresh oregano
coarse salt and freshly ground pepper
10 6-inch corn or flour tortillas

Mash beans in a medium bowl until chunky. Add goat cheese, tomato, corn, mango, onion, cilantro and oregano. Season with salt and pepper; stir until well combined.

Heat a grill pan or BBQ over medium heat. Spread 1/2 cup bean mixture evenly over 1 tortilla, and top with another tortilla. Repeat with remaining bean mixture and tortillas.

Grill quesadillas until grill marks appear and filling is hot, about 2 minutes per side. Cut into wedges and serve warm.

Soups

Soups

Cold Fruit Soup

1 16 ounce package frozen strawberries or any other frozen fruit
1 cup orange juice
1 tablespoon sugar
fresh mint as garnish

Thaw fruit for 5 to 10 minutes. Purée all ingredients together in a blender or food processor. Serve immediately.

For a beautiful presentation, pick two different fruits (different colors, i.e. strawberries and peaches) following the same recipe, in different batches. Using two ladles, at the same time, pour each batch into a bowl. Half will be pink and half will be orange.

Variation: Add vodka, gin or tequila for parties.

Watermelon Gazpacho

7 cups seedless watermelon, cubed
1 hothouse cucumber, peeled and rough chopped
4 roma tomatoes, seeded
1 small jalapeño chili, seeded
1 bunch fresh mint leaves, no stems, divided
balsamic vinegar, to taste
1/8 teaspoon salt
1/8 teaspoon pepper
1/8 teaspoon sugar
crème fraîche or pareve sour cream

In a food processor (depending on the capacity), add watermelon, cucumber and tomatoes. Add chili (only use half if you don't want the heat) and half the mint. Process until smooth.

Add balsamic vinegar in small spoonfuls, until you can lightly taste it. Add salt, pepper and sugar to finish. Taste. Serve chilled using small cups. Top with mint sprig and a swirl of crème fraîche or pareve sour cream.

Variation: It is also great spiked with vodka or rum.

Asparagus Soup

Yield: 8 1-cup servings
Prep Time: 40 minutes

2 tablespoons margarine
2 medium onions, chopped
2 leeks, chopped
6 cups chicken broth or low-sodium canned soup
2 pounds asparagus, ends trimmed, cut into 4 pieces
salt and pepper
pareve sour cream
croutons, garnish
mint leaves

Melt margarine in large pot over medium heat. Add onions and leeks, sauté until tender, about 15 minutes. Add chicken broth and asparagus, simmer until asparagus is tender, about 30 to 45 minutes. Purée soup in blender or processor in batches. Return to pot. Season with salt and pepper. Can be made one day ahead. Cover and chill. Bring to simmer before serving, stirring occasionally. Decorate with dollop of pareve sour cream. Add croutons or mint leaf.

Broccoli Soup

1 large onion, chopped
1 Golden Delicious apple, peeled and chopped
5 bouillon cubes
5 cups water
4 to 5 stalks broccoli, including florets
fresh or powdered garlic to taste

Sauté onion and apple until limp, not brown. Add bouillon and water. Cut up broccoli (especially the stem) and cook until fork soft. Put all in blender (except liquid) to purée. Add garlic. Return to pot with liquid and mix all together. Serve hot.

Easy Broccoli Soup

1 tablespoon olive or vegetable oil
2 medium yellow onions (2 cups), coarsely chopped
3 to 5 cloves garlic, slivered
1 1/4 pounds broccoli, cut into florets, stalks trimmed, peeled and thinly sliced, or 2 10 ounce packages frozen broccoli
3 medium all-purpose potatoes (1 pound), peeled and cut into cubes
1/4 teaspoon ground nutmeg
5 cups pareve chicken broth
2 cups low-fat milk or mocha mix
salt and pepper, to taste
2 green onions, sliced
3 tablespoons fresh parsley, minced, optional

In a large saucepan, heat oil over low heat. Add onions; cook, stirring frequently, for 5 minutes or until softened. Add garlic; cook for 30 seconds.

Add broccoli, potatoes, nutmeg and pareve chicken broth; bring to a boil over moderate heat. Adjust heat so mixture simmers gently. Cover; cook for 20 minutes or until broccoli and potatoes are very tender.

In a food processor or blender, working in batches if necessary, process mixture until puréed. Return purée to pot, stir in milk, salt and pepper; set over moderate heat for 4 minutes or just until heated through. Garnish with sliced green onions.

Optional: Garnish with fresh parsley

Corn Soup

1 large onion, chopped
1 tablespoon vegetable oil
1 yellow pepper, chopped
1 orange pepper, chopped
2 11 ounce cans yellow corn, drained
2 14 ounce cans vegetable broth
salt and pepper, to taste
dash of hot sauce, optional
1 11 ounce can Mexicorn
2 tablespoons chopped chives

Sauté onion in oil. Add peppers and yellow corn; cook until tender, approximately 5 minutes. Add broth; bring to a boil. Add salt, pepper and hot sauce. Simmer 10 minutes. Purée until smooth.

To serve: Drain and warm Mexicorn, spoon a couple of tablespoons in soup bowl and add puréed soup. Sprinkle with chives.

Roasted Carrot Ginger Soup

1 1/2 pounds carrots, peeled and halved lengthwise
1 pound parsnips, peeled and quartered lengthwise
1 large onion, sliced
2 inch piece of fresh ginger, peeled and chopped
6 tablespoons butter or margarine
3 tablespoons packed brown sugar
8 cups chicken broth or vegetarian broth, divided
salt and pinch of cayenne pepper
crème fraîche, to taste (omit if using chicken broth)
chives, sliced
shredded carrots, to taste

Preheat oven to 350 degrees. Combine carrots, parsnips, onion and ginger in a shallow roasting pan. Dot with butter or margarine. Sprinkle with brown sugar. Pour 2 cups broth into pan, cover well; bake until vegetables are tender, about 2 hours. Transfer vegetables and broth to large soup pot; add 6 more cups broth. Season with salt and cayenne pepper. Bring to a boil, reduce heat and simmer, partially covered for 10 minutes. Purée soup; add more broth, if desired. Serve with crème fraîche and chives or shredded carrots.

Carrot Zucchini Soup with Cumin

Yield: Serves 8

1 tablespoon olive oil
1 onion, chopped
2 stalks celery, chopped
1 teaspoon ground cumin
1/4 teaspoon turmeric
1/4 teaspoon nutmeg
1 pound carrots, peeled and sliced in rounds
2 zucchini, sliced in rounds
2 parsnips, peeled and sliced in rounds
6 cups chicken or vegetable broth
1 1/2 cups soy milk
salt
ground pepper
fresh cilantro, chopped for garnish

Heat olive oil in large pot over medium heat. Add onion and celery. Sauté until translucent, not brown. Add cumin, turmeric and nutmeg to onions. Mix for 2 minutes. Add carrots, zucchini and parsnips. Stir periodically for next 5 minutes. Add broth and simmer for 20 minutes, uncovered. Turn off heat. Mix with immersion blender in pot. Add soy milk. Season with salt and pepper, to taste. Garnish with fresh cilantro.

Note: Can be made vegetarian or meat. Can be prepared ahead and then warmed.

Cream of Mushroom Soup

Yield: Serves 5

1 medium onion, chopped
1 tablespoon butter
2 cups mushrooms, chopped
1 tablespoon flour
2 cups whole milk
salt and pepper, to taste
3 tablespoons cream
2 tablespoons sherry

Sauté onions in butter. Add mushrooms; cook until most of moisture is cooked away. Stir in flour; blend well with wooden spoon. Add milk; stir until thickened. Season with salt and pepper. Before serving, add cream and sherry.

Potato Leek Soup

6 leeks, sliced
2 to 3 garlic cloves, crushed
3 tablespoons olive oil
3 white potatoes, peeled and diced
2 32 ounce boxes vegetable broth
1 to 2 teaspoons turmeric, or to taste
salt and white pepper, to taste
1 bunch cilantro, chopped, optional, or add as garnish

Sauté leeks and garlic in olive oil until soft, not brown. Add potatoes, broth, turmeric, salt and white pepper. Simmer until potatoes are soft, about 45 minutes. Purée in blender or food processor. Then add cilantro and stir.

Sweet Potato Chipotle Soup

1 to 2 carrots
1 yellow onion
4 cloves garlic
3 large yams or sweet potatoes, peeled and cut into small pieces (reserve 1/2 cup)
1/2 to 1 cup real maple syrup (to taste)
vegetable oil
1 to 2 teaspoons salt
2 to 3 cups pareve chicken or vegetable broth, warm
1 chipotle pepper, seeded and finely chopped
1/2 to 1 teaspoon pepper
sour cream or plain yogurt, optional

Finely chop carrots, onion, garlic and 1/2 cup of sweet potatoes/yams. Sauté slowly in nonstick pan over medium-low heat until all are browned. Add maple syrup; simmer 5 to 10 minutes more, but before maple syrup evaporates too much. Boil remaining sweet potatoes/yams in water until soft. Add salt. Drain about 1/2 of water, leaving approximately 1 to 2 cups water with sweet potatoes/yams. Add frying pan ingredients, broth and chipotle pepper to sweet potatoes/yams/water. Add 1/2 to 1 teaspoon pepper or more, to taste. Simmer for 15 to 20 minutes. Let cool, then purée in blender. If too thick, add more broth or water to thin. Serve as is, or add a dollop of sour cream or plain yogurt (will temper heat of chipotle!).

Janice's Butternut Squash Soup

Yield: Serves 12-15

3 pounds butternut squash, peeled, seeded and cubed
1 onion, chopped
4 garlic cloves, chopped
2 potatoes, peeled and cubed
3 tomatoes, peeled, seeded and cubed or 1 14.5 ounce can peeled, chopped tomatoes
2 tablespoons fresh parsley, chopped
2 bay leaves
1 teaspoon fresh thyme
1 teaspoon fresh marjoram
2 tablespoons olive oil
salt and pepper to taste

Combine all ingredients. Add enough water to cover mixture. Bring to a boil. Reduce heat, simmer partially covered for about 40 minutes. Purée and serve.

Hint: Parboil squash for 5 minutes before peeling, or buy already peeled and cubed.

Banana Squash Soup

1 onion, chopped
2 tablespoons olive oil
2 to 3 garlic cloves, chopped
2 stalks celery, diced
1 large carrot, peeled and diced
1 medium leek (white part only), sliced into circles
2 pounds banana squash, peeled and diced
1 parsnip, peeled and diced, optional
1 rutabaga, peeled and diced
1/2 cup chopped parsley, optional
6 to 8 cups chicken broth
1 tablespoon curry powder
1/2 teaspoon ginger
1 to 2 teaspoons cumin
1 teaspoon white pepper
1 tablespoon sugar
2 teaspoons granulated garlic
1 bay leaf
salt, to taste

Sauté onions in olive oil. When onions start to wilt, add garlic. Add celery and carrots; continue to sauté. Add leeks, squash, parsnips, rutabaga and parsley; continue to sauté until vegetables start to wilt. Place vegetables in large stock pot; add chicken broth, seasonings and bay leaf. Bring soup to a boil, then cover and simmer until vegetables are tender. Remove from heat and cool. When cool, purée soup in a blender. Can be made up to 2 days in advance.

Butternut Squash Soup

1 large onion, sliced
2 tablespoons oil
3 pounds butternut squash, peeled and cubed
1 potato, peeled and cubed
5 cups chicken or vegetable broth
1/8 teaspoon cayenne or red pepper
1 teaspoon curry powder
1 teaspoon sugar
dash of nutmeg
1/2 cup soy milk
1 red bell pepper

Sauté onion in oil until golden. Add butternut squash and potatoes. Cook 2 minutes. Boil broth in large stock pot; add vegetables. Cook for 30 minutes covered. Season with cayenne or red pepper, curry powder and sugar. When cooked, purée. Add a good dash of nutmeg. Add soy milk; continue cooking. Roast red bell pepper, remove skin, purée. Drizzle on top of soup.

Tortilla Soup

6 corn tortillas
3 tablespoons virgin olive oil
1 red bell pepper, chopped
1 yellow bell pepper, chopped
4 stalks celery, sliced
1 medium onion, chopped
1 tablespoon chopped fresh garlic
1 gallon (16 cups) pareve chicken or vegetable broth
1 tablespoon ground cumin
2 cups canned tomato juice
1 teaspoon hot sauce (or to taste)
small dollop of sour cream, garnish
chopped cilantro, garnish
1/2 cup shredded Cheddar cheese
1 cup tortilla chips

Cut tortillas into 1/2 inch strips. Heat oil in large pot until it begins to smoke, then add tortilla strips and brown lightly. Add vegetables and garlic; sauté approximately 5 minutes, until soft. Add broth, cumin, tomato juice and hot sauce. Bring to a boil over high heat. Reduce heat to medium-high and boil about 2 hours to reduce soup by half.

Place in food processor (or blender) in batches and purée. Reheat; serve with garnish. Put small dollop of sour cream in center and chopped cilantro on top, shredded cheese around sour cream and chips on the side of the bowl, just touching the soup.

Zucchini Basil Soup

Yield: Serves 4

1 tablespoon olive oil
1 large yellow onion, chopped
2 pounds zucchini, sliced 1/4 inch thick
4 cups reduced-sodium vegetable broth
1 cup basil leaves, stemmed, loosely packed
1/4 cup fat-free half-and-half
1/4 teaspoon chili powder
sea salt, to taste
1/2 cup nonfat Greek yogurt
fresh chopped basil, for garnish

Heat olive oil in large saucepan over medium heat. Add onion; cook until translucent; about 5 minutes. Add zucchini; cook another 2 minutes before adding vegetable broth and basil leaves. Reduce heat to simmer; cook 20 minutes. Purée soup in batches in blender; return to saucepan to reheat. Add half-and-half. Add chili powder; season with salt, to taste. Garnish with spoonful of yogurt and fresh basil to serve.

Zucchini Soup

1 large onion, chopped
2 tablespoons olive oil or margarine or butter
2 stalks celery with leaves, chopped
6 to 8 medium zucchini, quartered lengthwise and chopped
1 large potato, peeled and chopped into 1/2 inch pieces
1 tablespoon dried dill or 1/2 cup fresh snipped dill
5 cups vegetable broth (or bouillon)
1 teaspoon salt (or to taste)
garlic, to taste
1/2 teaspoon freshly ground pepper

Heat olive oil in a large soup pot; sauté onion until translucent. Add celery; sauté until soft, about 5 minutes. Add zucchini, potato, dill, broth, salt, garlic and pepper. Heat to boiling, cover; turn heat down. Simmer soup for 35 minutes until vegetables are soft. When cooled slightly, purée using an immersion blender or remove to blender; purée in batches. You can make this soup very smooth, or leave slightly chunky; good either way.

Tuscan Bean Soup

Yield: Serves 6

2 tablespoons olive oil
1 medium onion, chopped
2 stalks celery, chopped
2 medium carrots, peeled and sliced
3 cloves garlic, crushed and minced
1 teaspoon salt
1/2 teaspoon pepper
2 to 3 teaspoons dried basil
2 15 ounce cans cannellini or white northern beans
2 1/2 to 3 cups water or vegetable broth
Parmesan cheese, to taste
minced parsley, optional

In a large soup pot, heat olive oil; sauté onion, celery, carrots and garlic over medium heat for 5 minutes. Season with salt, pepper and basil, Cover, turn heat way down and cook gently 10 minutes more. Add beans (including liquid) and water or broth; cover and simmer for 30 minutes. If soup seems too thick, add more liquid. Serve topped with Parmesan cheese and parsley.

Chilled Cucumber and Tomato Soup with Fresh Dill

Yield: Serves 8

1 quart low-fat plain yogurt
2 cups pareve chicken or vegetable broth
1 large seedless cucumber, peeled, leaving some of green skin on, diced and lightly salted
2 medium plum tomatoes, diced and lightly salted
1/4 cup extra-virgin olive oil
1 tablespoon wine vinegar
1 tablespoon rice vinegar
2 teaspoons chopped fresh dill
salt and ground black pepper, to taste

Mix all ingredients in a large bowl. Season to taste with salt and pepper.
Serve or refrigerate until ready to serve.

Gazpacho

1 to 3 cloves garlic, peeled
4 ripe tomatoes, sliced
1/2 green pepper, seeded and sliced
1 onion, peeled and sliced (use more or less)
1 slim cucumber, peeled and sliced
1 teaspoon salt
1/4 teaspoon pepper
2 tablespoons olive oil
3 tablespoons white wine vinegar
1/2 cup ice water
2 scallions, sliced, garnish

Put all ingredients in a blender or food processor, except scallions. Blend 5 to 10 seconds until finely chopped. Chill thoroughly, serve in bowls. Garnish with any of the above vegetables and scallions.

If too strong, add another tomato.

Make-Ahead Gazpacho

1 46 ounce can tomato juice
1 cup water
2 to 3 cloves garlic
1 onion
2 stalks celery and some leaves
1/2 cup parsley
1 green pepper
1 cucumber, peeled
3 ripe tomatoes
juice of 1 lemon
1 tablespoon red wine vinegar
1 teaspoon hot sauce
salt and pepper, to taste

Pour tomato juice and water into large container. Chop garlic by dropping it into a dry moving food processor. Add onion and chop. Mix onion and garlic with tomato juice. Chop celery, parsley, green pepper, cucumber and tomatoes separately in food processor and add to juice. Add lemon juice, red wine vinegar and hot sauce. Season with salt and pepper. Chill for several hours.

Serve in bowls with garnish of chopped olives, chives and croutons.

Hint: Can make one day ahead.

Pareve Gazpacho

Yield: Serves 6-8

1 bunch cilantro, washed and stems removed
3 ripe tomatoes
3 stalks celery
1 red pepper
2 hothouse cucumbers, peeled
1 clove garlic
1 46 ounce can tomato juice
1 teaspoon hot pepper sauce
1 teaspoon sugar
juice of one lemon
1 tablespoon red wine vinegar
1 tablespoon olive oil
1/2 teaspoon ground cumin
salt and pepper, to taste
extra cucumber, sliced, garnish

Finely chop cilantro and set aside in a very large bowl. Finely chop tomatoes, celery, red pepper, cucumbers and garlic, by hand or in food processor. Combine chopped vegetables in large bowl with cilantro. Add tomato juice, hot pepper sauce, sugar, lemon juice, red wine vinegar, olive oil and cumin. Season to taste with salt and pepper. Mix well and chill 3 hours. Serve garnished with cucumber slices.

Tip: Chopping by hand will give a coarse, salsa-like texture. For a smoother texture use a food processor, but do not over-process.

Lentil Soup, Susan-Style

Yield: Serves 6

2 tablespoons olive oil
1 large onion, chopped
1 stalk celery, chopped
1 carrot, peeled and chopped fine
1 parsnip, peeled and chopped fine
1/4 cup minced parsley
1/2 teaspoon dried thyme
1/2 teaspoon dried marjoram
1/4 teaspoon turmeric
1 15 ounce can diced tomatoes with juice
1 cup brown lentils, picked over and rinsed
1/4 cup dry sherry
4 cups water
1 teaspoon salt
1/2 teaspoon pepper
grated Cheddar or Swiss cheese, garnish

In large soup pot, heat olive oil; sauté onion, celery, carrot and parsnip until soft, about 7 minutes. Add parsley, thyme, marjoram, turmeric; sauté another 3 minutes. Add tomatoes with juice, lentils, sherry and water. Bring to boil, turn heat down, cover and cook 45 minutes. Check and add more water, if needed. Cook another 10 minutes. Season with salt and pepper. Serve topped with grated Cheddar or Swiss cheese.

Moroccan-Style Matzo Ball Soup

Yield: Serves 8

2 tablespoons olive oil
1 medium onion, minced
2 large or 3 medium leeks, white parts only, quartered lengthwise and chopped
2 medium potatoes, peeled and diced
3 medium white turnips, peeled and diced
3 medium carrots, peeled and sliced
3 medium stalks celery, diced
1/2 pound mushrooms, chopped
8 cups vegetable broth or water, or a combination
1 teaspoon paprika
1 teaspoon ground cumin, optional
1 pound can garbanzo beans (chickpeas), drained and rinsed, optional
salt and pepper, to taste
2 cups frozen peas
matzo balls

Heat oil in large soup pot. Add onion and leeks, sauté over medium heat until leeks are limp, about 10 minutes. Add potatoes, turnips, carrots, celery, mushrooms, broth or water, paprika and cumin, mix well. Bring to a boil, lower heat and simmer gently until vegetables are tender, about 45 minutes. Add garbanzo beans (optional), salt and pepper; simmer 10 minutes more. Stir in frozen peas. Cover and let stand several hours or overnight in refrigerator to develop flavors. Reheat before serving. Serve with matzo balls.

Hint: Matzo balls can be cooked in soup.

Fast and Easy Minestrone Soup

2 tablespoons olive oil
1 bunch green onions, chopped
2 packages dried vegetable soup
1 15 ounce can tomato sauce
1 10 ounce package frozen chopped spinach, thawed and drained
1 teaspoon basil
1 teaspoon oregano
8 cups hot water
1/2 cup small uncooked macaroni
Parmesan cheese, optional

In a 4-quart or larger soup pot, sauté green onions in olive oil, until soft. Add rest of ingredients, except Parmesan cheese; bring to boil. Let simmer, partially covered, about 30 minutes. Stir occasionally. Serve with Parmesan cheese.

Lillian's Minestrone Soup

Yield: Serves 8

1/4 cup olive oil
2 cloves garlic, minced
1 large onion, finely chopped
3 tablespoons fresh parsley, finely chopped
1 teaspoon dried thyme
2 teaspoons dried basil
1 tablespoon tomato paste
1/4 cup water
3 celery stalks, chopped
2 carrots, peeled and diced
2 medium potatoes, peeled and diced
2 zucchini, diced
3 tomatoes, chopped
5 cups vegetable broth
salt and pepper, to taste
1 cup small elbow or shell shaped pasta, uncooked
1 1/2 cups cooked beans: cannellini, garbanzo or red kidney
Parmesan cheese, shredded, garnish

Heat olive oil in a large soup pot. Add garlic, onion, parsley, thyme and basil, sauté until soft, about 5 minutes. Add tomato paste, thinned with 1/4 cup water and cook over low heat 4 minutes more. Add celery, carrots, potatoes, zucchini, tomatoes and broth. Salt and pepper, to taste. Bring to a soft boil, cover and lower heat. Simmer soup for 45 minutes. Bring back to a boil, add pasta, reduce heat slightly and cook 10 minutes more. Add cooked beans and heat another 5 minutes. Serve with Parmesan cheese and crusty bread.

Tomato Soup with Dumplings

Yield: Serves 6

TOMATO SOUP
- 1 48 ounce can tomato juice
- 1/2 can water
- sugar, to taste
- dash cinnamon

Bring all to a boil and add nuckerly (dumplings).

NUCKERLY (DUMPLINGS)
- 1 egg
- 1/3 cup water
- 1 shake of salt
- 3/4 cup flour

Mix nuckerly ingredients together. Heat a spoon in soup and scoop 'gnocchi' sized mixture, then drop into soup. Simmer 45 minutes. Particularly good with tomato soup.

Tomato Rice Soup

Yield: Serves 10

- 2 teaspoons olive oil
- 1 medium onion, finely chopped
- 2 medium carrots, peeled and finely chopped
- 1 medium fresh fennel bulb, finely chopped
- 2 ribs celery, finely chopped
- 1 14 ounce can chopped Italian-style tomatoes
- 8 cups vegetable broth
- 1/2 cup Arborio rice
- 1/4 cup finely chopped cilantro
- 1/4 cup finely chopped basil leaves
- kosher salt, to taste
- white pepper, to taste

Heat oil in large saucepan and sauté onion, carrots, fennel and celery until soft. Stir in tomatoes and broth. Bring to low boil. Then reduce heat to simmer; partially cover saucepan; simmer 25 to 30 minutes. Stir in rice and cook until tender, about 20 minutes longer. Next add cilantro and basil, season with salt and pepper. If soup thickens too much, add more broth and adjust seasonings.

Chicken Barley Soup

Yield: Serves 4

1 chicken, cut-up
1 onion
10 cups water
2 stalks celery, sliced
2 to 3 carrots, peeled and sliced
1 parsnip, peeled and chopped
1 cup fresh parsley, chopped
7 ounces canned diced tomatoes
3/4 to 1 cup barley
salt and pepper, to taste

Cook chicken parts and onion in water, approximately 45 minutes. Add celery, carrots, parsnips, parsley and tomatoes; cook another 30 minutes. Add barley; cook an additional 30 minutes, or until barley is done. Add salt and pepper, to taste.

Variation: A little tomato juice can be added instead of the diced tomatoes for flavor and color.

Leora's Chicken Soup

Yield: Serves 6

1 bunch Italian parsley, chopped
4 to 5 inner stalks celery with leaves, chopped
1 tomato, seeded and chopped
4 cups chicken broth
2/3 cup fine noodles
salt and pepper, to taste

In a large soup pot, add vegetables to broth, bring to a boil. Cover, lower heat and simmer for 15 minutes. Add noodles, simmer another 10 minutes. Add salt and pepper, to taste.

Variation: Add onion and garlic to taste.

Mexican Chicken Soup

Yield: Serves 10

1 4 1/2 to 5 pound chicken, cut-up
10 cups water
1/2 onion, sliced
3 stalks celery, cut up
1 teaspoon salt
1/8 teaspoon pepper
1 16 ounce can tomatoes, cut up
3 medium carrots, peeled and thinly sliced (1 1/2 cups)
1 medium onion, chopped
1 small zucchini, thinly sliced (4 ounces)
1 cup frozen peas
1 small avocado, peeled, seeded and sliced

In Dutch oven, combine chicken, water, onion, celery, salt and pepper. Simmer, covered, for 2 hours until chicken is tender. Remove chicken from broth. Strain broth and discard vegetables. Return broth to pot. Add undrained tomatoes, carrots and onion; simmer covered for 30 minutes or until carrots are tender. Meanwhile, cool chicken to handle, remove skin and bones. Cube chicken, add to broth with zucchini and peas. Cover and simmer 10 to 15 minutes longer until vegetables are tender. Just before serving, garnish with avocado slices.

Variation: Add one Anaheim chili, grilled, peeled and chopped. No seeds. Add tortilla chips.

Rose's Mushroom Barley Soup

2 knuckle bones with meat or short ribs
10 cups water
1 large onion, diced
2 stalks celery, diced
1 package minestrone soup (found in kosher aisle of market)
21 tablespoons (big) barley
1 16 ounce bag frozen peas
1 tablespoon salt (or to taste)
1 potato, peeled and diced
1 bay leaf
pepper, to taste
1/2 pound mushrooms, sliced
2 carrots, peeled and sliced
1 16 ounce bag mixed vegetables
1 tablespoon parsley flakes

Boil bones in the water for 10 to 15 minutes and remove scum (white foam).
Add remaining ingredients and cook an additional 45 minutes.

Taco Soup

Yield: Serves 8

1 1/2 pounds turkey, ground
1 package taco seasoning
2 cans corn nibs with juice
2 cans diced tomatoes with juice
2 cans chili beans with juice
crushed tortilla chips

Heat first 5 ingredients for 15 minutes. Put crushed tortilla chips on bottom of individual soup bowls. Pour soup on top. Enjoy!

Carrot Soup

Yield: Serves 12-15

1 onion, chopped
vegetable oil
4 to 6 medium carrots, diced
4 cups chicken/vegetable broth
1/4 teaspoon lemon peel
1/2 teaspoon salt
1 teaspoon curry powder
2 tablespoons pareve margarine
1 teaspoon sugar
1/8 teaspoon white pepper
3 tablespoons sherry

Sauté onions in oil until translucent; add all ingredients, except sherry. Cover; simmer until soft. Cool; put in blender/processor. Add sherry.

Borscht Parfait

Yield: Serves 12

BORSCHT
2 envelopes kosher gelatin
1 quart borscht
1/4 cup cold water
juice of 1/2 lemon
1 tablespoon onion juice
1 tablespoon finely chopped onions
1 teaspoon fresh chopped dill
2 dashes hot pepper sauce

DRESSING
1/2 cup sour cream
1 tablespoon lemon juice
1 teaspoon white wine vinegar
2 dashes hot pepper sauce
sour cream, garnish
dill, garnish

Soften gelatin in cold water. Dissolve in hot borscht. Cool slightly; add remaining borscht ingredients. Pour in 9×13 pan; chill in refrigerator until firm. Mix dressing ingredients, except for garnishes. Cut chilled borscht into cubes; arrange in parfait glasses, alternating with dressing. Top with dollop of sour cream and sprinkle of dill.

Salads

Salads

Pickled Beets

- 1/4 cup sugar
- 2 tablespoons vinegar
- 1 tablespoon cornstarch
- 2 cups beet juice, drained from canned beets
- 1/4 teaspoon salt
- 2 cans beets

Over a low flame, mix everything together, except beets, until liquid gets clear and thick. Add beets. Cool and refrigerate.

Broccoli Salad

Yield: Serves 10

SALAD

- 2 bunches broccoli, chopped (cut off most of stems)
- 3/4 cup chopped red onion
- 1 cup raisins, mixed dark and yellow
- 1 cup shelled sunflower seeds

DRESSING

- 1 cup light mayonnaise
- 2 tablespoons red wine vinegar
- 1/4 to 1/2 cup sugar

Mix salad ingredients. Set aside. Mix dressing ingredients and combine with salad.

Moroccan Carrot Salad

1 1/2 pounds carrots, washed, peeled and sliced
1 garlic clove, finely chopped
1/2 cup vegetable oil
1 teaspoon dried red pepper flakes
1 teaspoon sweet paprika
3/4 cup water
1 teaspoon salt
1/2 teaspoon turmeric
1/3 cup vinegar
1 tablespoon lemon juice
1 tablespoon chopped fresh parsley

Lightly boil carrots until they are tender, but still firm. Drain them and allow to cool. Gently sauté garlic in oil until soft and translucent, about 5 minutes. Add red pepper flakes and paprika to pan and sauté for 1 minute. Slowly pour in water, then add cooked carrots, salt, turmeric, vinegar and lemon juice and simmer for 5 minutes. Remove from heat, allow to cool. Cover and refrigerate for 24 hours. Stir well before serving, sprinkle with parsley. Serve cold.

Chinese Salad and Dressing

Yield: Serves 8-10 as a side dish or 4-5 as a main dish

SALAD

2 heads romaine lettuce, cut or torn
1 tablespoon roasted sesame seeds, optional
3 scallions, cut fine
1 2.25 ounce package of sliced almonds, toasted
1/2 of 5 ounce can chow mein noodles
3/4 of 11 ounce can Mandarin oranges, drained very well
3 1/2 pounds boneless chicken breasts, cooked and diced

Combine all ingredients in a large bowl. Pour dressing over salad before serving. This salad can be made as a Chinese Chicken Salad or just a Chinese Salad without the chicken.

DRESSING

2 teaspoons sugar
1/3 cup vegetable oil
1 tablespoon dark sesame oil
3 tablespoons seasoned rice vinegar
1/4 teaspoon lite soy sauce

Combine all in a jar and shake well. Refrigerate for at least a few hours (overnight is fine).
Shake before using.

Creamy Summer Mediterranean Salad

SALAD

7 tomatoes
5 green onions
7 Persian cucumbers
1 1/2 green peppers
1/2 head romaine or red lettuce

Chop into large or small chunks as desired.

DRESSING

1 cup cottage cheese
1 cup sour cream
salt and pepper

Mix cottage cheese and sour cream together; add salt and pepper to taste.
Mix dressing and salad together.

Detroit Salad

SALAD

1/2 pound baby Swiss cheese, cut in 1/4 inch cubes
2 tart apples, cut in small pieces
8 ounces fresh mushrooms, sliced
1 large head romaine lettuce, torn
1 cup cashews, toasted

Combine all of the above ingredients. Dressing can be made ahead and poured over salad when served.

DRESSING

1 cup salad oil
3/4 cup sugar
1/3 cup red wine vinegar
dash of salt
1 tablespoon Dijon mustard
1 tablespoon grated onion
1 1/2 tablespoons poppy seeds

Place all ingredients in blender and blend until well mixed. Do not refrigerate.
Use salad dressing sparingly.

Fruited Romaine Salad with Lemon Poppy Seed Dressing

Yield: Serves 12

SALAD

- 1 large head romaine lettuce, torn into bite-size pieces
- 1 cup cashews, lightly salted
- 1/4 cup dried, sweetened cranberries
- 1 to 2 Gala apples, cubed
- 1 to 2 D'Anjou pears, cubed

DRESSING

- 1/2 cup sugar
- 1/3 cup lemon juice
- 2 teaspoons finely chopped onion
- 1 teaspoon Dijon mustard
- 1/2 teaspoon salt
- 2/3 cup oil
- 1 tablespoon poppy seeds

In a blender, combine sugar, lemon juice, onion, mustard and salt. Cover and blend. While blender is still running, add oil in a slow, steady stream. Continue to blend until thick and smooth. Add poppy seeds and blend until mixed. In a large bowl, combine all the salad ingredients. Toss to mix. Add dressing.

Tip: Apples and pears can be peeled or not, according to your preference.

Israeli Salad

- equal parts tomatoes and kirbies (cucumbers)
- olive or vegetable oil
- lemon juice, optional
- salt
- pepper
- garlic powder

Dice vegetables into 1-inch pieces. Toss with enough oil to coat and seasonings to taste. Refrigerate no more than 30 minutes before serving. This salad doesn't keep well, so only make as much as you will need for one meal.

Linda's Salad

Yield: Serves 20

SALAD

4 8 ounce bags baby greens (spring mix)
1 1/2 ounces pine nuts, toasted
6 ounces dried, sweetened cranberries
1/4 pound goat cheese, crumbled
additional Parmesan cheese, to taste

Combine all ingredients in a large bowl. Pour dressing over salad before serving. Use dressing sparingly. This makes more dressing than you'll need.

DRESSING

2 garlic cloves
1/2 cup lemon juice
1 1/3 cups vegetable oil
2/3 cup Parmesan cheese
3/4 teaspoon salt
1/2 teaspoon black pepper
2 teaspoons soy sauce
1/4 cup sliced green onions

Combine and blend all of the above ingredients, except green onions. Stir in green onions (taste for more lemon juice or soy sauce).

Patti's Yummy Salad

Yield: Serves 8

1 head romaine lettuce (red leaf and/or butter lettuce are nice to mix in as well)
1 1/2 to 2 cups grilled or canned corn
1 cup grated carrots
1 11 ounce can Mandarin orange slices
1 cup dried, sweetened cranberries
1 cup honey glazed pecans
Champagne vinaigrette dressing

Combine first 6 ingredients in large bowl; toss with dressing.

Variation: Add other vegetables per your preference: cherry tomatoes, avocado, bell pepper, cucumbers, etc.

Mediterranean Salad

Yield: Serves 6-8

1 15 ounce can garbanzo beans, drained and rinsed
4 roma tomatoes, quartered
1 cucumber, peeled, halved lengthwise and sliced
1/2 cup crumbled feta cheese
3 green onions, sliced
1 cup Kalamata or Nicoise olives (preferably pitted)
1/4 cup lemon juice
1/4 cup olive oil
1/4 cup chopped parsley
1 teaspoon dried basil (or 2 tablespoons chopped fresh)
1 teaspoon zaatar (found in kosher or Israeli markets)
2 tablespoons red wine vinegar
salt and pepper
6 to 8 large romaine lettuce leaves

Mix garbanzo beans, tomatoes, cucumber, feta, green onions and olives in a large salad bowl. Refrigerate. Mix lemon juice, olive oil, parsley, basil, zaatar, vinegar, salt and pepper to taste, in small mixing bowl. Just before serving, arrange 1 lettuce leaf on each plate. Toss salad with dressing and serve on lettuce leaf, or line salad bowl with lettuce leaves, spoon tossed salad on top. If making ahead of time, store vegetables and dressing separately.

Super Salad

Yield: Serves 12

mixture of favorite lettuces, suggest: romaine and butter lettuce
2 cups shredded carrots
10 ounces grape tomatoes
2 cups frozen grilled corn, defrosted
1 11 ounce can Mandarin orange slices
6 ounces dried, sweetened cranberries
2 1/2 ounces honey-roasted pecans
1 red bell pepper, diced
1 yellow bell pepper, diced
1 English cucumber, skin on, sliced
diced avocado, optional
Champagne dressing

Mix all ingredients and serve immediately.

The World's Best Brunch Salad

Yield: Serves 4 as a side dish

CANDIED ALMONDS

3 tablespoons sugar
1/2 cup sliced almonds

Melt sugar in a large frying pan, stirring continuously. Pour almonds in; stir continuously until coated. Spread onto wax paper to cool.

SALAD

1/2 head green leaf lettuce, torn into pieces
1/2 head romaine lettuce, torn into pieces
1/2 cup chopped celery
4 chopped green onions
1 11 ounce can Mandarin oranges
1 avocado, cut into cubes
1 to 2 apples, diced (any kind)
1/4 to 1/2 cup dried cranberries
1/2 cup blue cheese, crumbled

SALAD DRESSING

1/2 teaspoon salt
1/2 teaspoon pepper
1/4 cup olive oil
1 tablespoon chopped parsley
2 tablespoons sugar
2 tablespoons white wine vinegar

Mix dressing separately. Combine salad ingredients in a bowl. Toss salad and candied almonds and pour dressing over salad.

Variation: You can substitute goat cheese for blue cheese.

Spinach, Apple and Dried, Sweetened Cranberry Salad

Yield: Serves 5-6

SALAD

1 6 ounce package baby spinach leaves
2/3 12 ounce package sliced apples (or 2 large apples, thinly sliced)
1/2 cup dried, sweetened cranberries
1/2 7 ounce package glazed pecans

Cut each slice of apple into quarters, creating a large dice. Mix all ingredients in a large bowl.

DRESSING

1/4 cup chopped onion
2 tablespoons apple cider vinegar
2 tablespoons white wine vinegar
1/4 teaspoon paprika
2 tablespoons sugar
1 teaspoon salt
1/4 teaspoon pepper
1/3 cup vegetable oil
2 tablespoons sesame seeds

Combine first 7 ingredients in a blender or food processor. While blender is running, slowly add oil. Pour into a container; mix in sesame seeds. Toss salad with dressing.

Mango Chutney Spinach Salad

Yield: Serves 12

1/2 cup vegetable oil
6 ounces mango chutney, large dice
1 teaspoon curry powder
1 teaspoon dry mustard
1/2 teaspoon lemon juice
1 pound steamed spinach
1 large Fuji or Granny Smith apple, cut into chunks
1 cup toasted spicy pecans
1/2 cup dried, sweetened cranberries or raisins
6 scallions, thinly sliced

Combine first 5 ingredients in a small bowl. Toss with spinach. Add next 4 ingredients. Mix and serve immediately.

Spinach and Cucumber Salad with Berries and Curry Dressing

Yield: Serves 8

SALAD

6 ounces fresh spinach (about 6 cups), torn into silver-dollar size pieces
4 Persian cucumbers (about 3/4 cup), thinly sliced
1 cup strawberries, thickly sliced
3/4 cup red raspberries
1 cup blueberries, trimmed
1 small red onion, thinly sliced
1/2 cup chopped pecans
1/4 cup sliced almonds

DRESSING

3 tablespoons vegetable oil
2 tablespoons rice vinegar
1 tablespoon balsamic vinegar
1 tablespoon plus 1 teaspoon honey
1 teaspoon curry powder
2 teaspoons Dijon mustard
salt and white pepper, to taste

Wash and dry spinach. Beat together dressing ingredients, then toss lightly with spinach and cucumbers. Add berries, onion, pecans and almonds. Toss lightly and serve immediately.

Spinach Salad with Mandarin Orange Dressing

Yield: Serves 4-6

SALAD

10 ounces baby spinach leaves
1/4 cup toasted sunflower seeds
2 11 ounce cans Mandarin orange segments, drained, divided
1/2 red onion, thinly sliced

Toss spinach, sunflower seeds, oranges (reserve 8 segments for dressing) and onion slices with dressing. Serve immediately.

MANDARIN ORANGE DRESSING

8 Mandarin orange segments, reserved from salad
1/4 cup vegetable oil
1 tablespoon plus 1 teaspoon sugar
1/2 teaspoon salt
2 tablespoons balsamic or red wine vinegar
2 to 3 dashes hot sauce

Purée orange segments in blender. Add oil, sugar, salt, vinegar and hot sauce until puréed. Makes 1/2 cup.

Layered Salad

Yield: Serves 12

SALAD

- 4 cups lettuce or spinach, shredded
- 2 cups mild Cheddar cheese, shredded, divided
- 1 1/2 cups mushrooms, sliced
- 1 small red onion, sliced and separated into rings
- 2 cups chopped plum tomatoes
- 2 hard-boiled eggs, thinly sliced
- 1 10 ounce package frozen peas, defrosted

DRESSING

- 1/2 cup mayonnaise
- 1/2 cup sour cream
- 1/4 cup chopped fresh basil
- 1 cup kosher imitation bacon bits

Layer spinach, 1 cup cheese, mushrooms, onions, tomatoes, eggs and peas in 3 quart serving bowl. Mix mayonnaise, sour cream and basil. Spread over salad to seal. Cover and refrigerate at least 5 hours or overnight. Sprinkle with remaining cheese and imitation bacon bits just before serving.

Cabbage Slaw

Yield: Serves 5

SLAW

- 4 cups grated cabbage
- 2 small carrots, shredded, optional
- 1 green pepper, shredded, optional

DRESSING

- 4 teaspoons vegetable oil
- 1/3 cup white vinegar
- 1/2 teaspoon dry mustard
- 1/2 teaspoon celery seeds
- 2 tablespoons sugar
- 4 teaspoons pimento, chopped
- 1 teaspoon salt
- 1/4 teaspoon pepper
- 1 teaspoon dehydrated onion flakes

Mix vegetables, set aside. Mix all dressing ingredients together. Pour over vegetables. Prepare a day ahead.

Health Slaw

Yield: Serves 6

SLAW

1 small head green cabbage
3 to 4 medium carrots
1 cucumber

DRESSING

1/4 cup white vinegar
1/4 cup water
1/4 cup sugar

Cut cabbage into sections to fit in a food processor with thin (2mm) slicing blade. Slice and remove to large bowl. Peel carrots and cucumber; slice in food processor with same blade. Toss all vegetables together in large bowl.

Combine vinegar, water and sugar in food processor with mixing blade. Whirl until combined. Pour over vegetables. Mix together.

Fried Chicken Cole Slaw

1 head cabbage (red or green)
1 carrot, optional
1/2 cup sugar
2 teaspoons salt, or to taste
1/4 cup balsamic vinegar (regular or white)
3 tablespoons vegetable oil
1 cup real mayonnaise

Shred cabbage and carrot (if using) and put in large bowl. In separate bowl, combine remaining ingredients; mix until blended. Pour dressing over cabbage, toss well to coat cabbage and carrots. Place in refrigerator for about 1 hour; mix before serving. Slaw can be made in the morning for a meal later in the day, but be sure to let it sit for 1 hour.

Can be easily doubled for large groups.

Red Cabbage Slaw

Yield: Serves 8
Prep Time: 10 Minutes

1 large head purple cabbage
1 large red onion
3/4 cup white balsamic vinegar
3/4 cup sugar
2 1/2 teaspoons salt
pepper, to taste
1/2 cup vegetable oil

Slice cabbage and onion very thinly. Bring vinegar, sugar, salt, pepper and oil to a boil. Cool slightly and pour over cabbage mixture. Refrigerate overnight and turn occasionally to give cabbage a bright purple color.

Couscous and Vegetable Salad

Yield: Serves 6

SALAD
8 ounces whole wheat couscous, cooked
3 cups arugula
2 cups vine-ripe tomatoes, diced
2 cups fresh cooked corn kernels, cut from cob
1/4 cup salted pumpkin seeds
1/3 cup dried, sweetened cranberries
1/3 cup Asiago cheese, grated
fresh basil leaves, garnish
1 avocado, diced, garnish

DRESSING
1/2 cup fresh, packed basil leaves
1/2 cup buttermilk
1/2 cup lite mayonnaise
2 teaspoons fresh lemon juice
1/2 teaspoon sea salt
1/2 teaspoon fresh black pepper

To make dressing: blend all ingredients in food processor or blender until smooth. Refrigerate until ready to use. In large salad bowl, mix couscous, arugula, tomatoes, corn, pumpkin seeds and cranberries. Toss with dressing right before serving. Sprinkle with Asiago cheese; garnish with fresh basil leaves and avocado.

Couscous Salad

Yield: Serves 8 as a side dish

SALAD

1 1/4 cups water
1 cup whole wheat couscous
2/3 cup dried mung beans
1 Persian cucumber, diced
1 large carrot, diced
1/2 red pepper, diced
1/4 cup currants
1/4 cup red onion, diced or green onion, sliced

In a large saucepan, bring water to a boil. Remove from heat; add couscous in a slow stream. Stir well, cover; let stand for 5 minutes. Fluff with a fork; set aside in a large mixing bowl to cool. In another saucepan, combine mung beans with water to cover; bring to a boil. Reduce heat; cook about 25 minutes or until tender, but not breaking apart. Drain in strainer; add to couscous. When couscous and mung beans are cool, add cucumber, carrot, pepper, currants and onion. Stir to combine.

DRESSING

1/2 teaspoon cumin
1/8 teaspoon cayenne pepper
1/4 teaspoon cinnamon
juice of 1 lemon
2 tablespoons olive oil
2 tablespoons rice wine vinegar

To make dressing, mix cumin, cayenne and cinnamon in a small bowl. Add lemon juice, olive oil and rice wine vinegar; whisk to blend. Pour over couscous mixture. Taste and adjust seasonings. Let rest for 1 hour.

Berry Couscous Salad

Yield: Serves 15

3 5.8 ounce packages roasted garlic & olive oil couscous, prepared as directed
1 16 ounce package frozen petite peas, thawed
1 16 ounce package frozen sweet petite corn, thawed
1 4 ounce box pine nuts
8 ounces combined:
golden raisins, dried cherries, dried, sweetened cranberries and dried blueberries
1/2 cup green onions, finely sliced
salt to taste

Once couscous is cooked and cooled, mix in other ingredients and serve.

Variation: Add Feta cheese.

Sesame Noodles Spicy Asian Pasta Salad

Yield: Serves 10

1 pound spaghetti or linguini, cooked al dente
1/4 cup sesame oil
1/3 cup soy sauce (can use low-sodium soy sauce)
2 tablespoons sugar
2 1/2 tablespoons red wine vinegar
2 teaspoons salt
1 cup chopped cilantro or Italian parsley
1 large red pepper, seeded and diced
8 to 10 green onions, slivered
1/2 cup peas or 1 cup sliced mushrooms or 1/2 cup sliced water chestnuts, optional
1 1/2 cups dry roasted peanuts or chili-flavored peanuts
toasted sesame seeds, to taste

Put cooked spaghetti in colander; rinse with cold water. Drain well; put in a large mixing bowl. In another bowl, combine sesame oil, soy sauce, sugar, vinegar and salt. Whisk until sugar has dissolved. Set aside. To spaghetti, add cilantro, peppers, green onions and peas, mushrooms or water chestnuts, if desired. Toss with dressing. Sprinkle peanuts and sesame seeds over salad before serving.

Variation: For spicier salad, add 1/8 teaspoon red pepper flakes in dressing.

Pasta Salad Roma

Yield: 6 cups

4 cups (8 ounce package) shell pasta, cooked, drained
2 14.5 ounce cans stewed tomatoes with juice
1 6 ounce jar artichoke hearts
1/2 cup pitted ripe olives
1/4 cup green onions, sliced
2 tablespoons chopped fresh basil
2 tablespoons chopped fresh oregano
2 tablespoons grated Parmesan (additional for garnish)
2 tablespoons wine vinegar
1/2 teaspoon salt
1/4 teaspoon red pepper flakes

Combine all ingredients. Chill thoroughly. Garnish with additional cheese.

Egg Salad

Yield: Serves 10

12 hard-boiled eggs
2 to 3 stalks celery
2 to 4 green onions
2 1/4 tablespoons mayonnaise
1 tablespoon Dijon mustard
1 1/2 teaspoons salt
1/2 teaspoon pepper

Chop eggs, 6 at a time, in food processor. Put in bowl. Chop celery and green onions. Mix with eggs. Add mayonnaise, mustard, salt and pepper. Mix well. Serve on lettuce leaves as salad or on bread for a delicious sandwich.

Oriental Curried Tuna Salad

2 12 ounce cans tuna fish, drained
2 8 ounce cans pineapple, drained; chopped into bite-size pieces (fresh is also fine)
2 8 ounce cans water chestnuts, chopped
1 cup chopped celery
1 10 ounce bag frozen peas, defrosted
1 1/2 cups mayonnaise
5 tablespoons sour cream
4 tablespoons curry powder, or more to taste
1 teaspoon garlic powder
1 5 ounce can chow mein noodles, divided

Mix tuna fish, pineapple, water chestnuts and celery together, breaking up tuna fish into appropriate bits. Fold in peas. Mix mayonnaise, sour cream, curry powder and garlic powder together. Add mayonnaise mixture to tuna and blend. Immediately prior to serving, add half of chow mein noodles to tuna mixture and top with remaining noodles as garnish.

Tuna Grape Waldorf Salad

Yield: Serves 6

1 1/2 cups seedless grapes (red and green), cut in half, divided
1 cup diced apples, unpeeled
1 7 ounce can tuna, drained
1/2 cup chopped pecans
1/2 cup mayonnaise
2 tablespoons fresh lemon juice
1 cup diced celery
1/4 cup dried onions or to taste

Combine 1 cup grapes with remaining ingredients, toss. Adjust mayonnaise and onions to taste. Top with 1/2 cup grapes for decoration.

Pea Chicken Salad

Yield: Serves 8
Prep Time: 15 minutes

1 20 ounce bag frozen peas, thawed and drained
1 16 ounce bag frozen stir-fry vegetables (the kind with no peppers in it), thawed and drained
1 cup thinly sliced celery
3/4 cup mayonnaise
1 1/2 teaspoons lemon juice
1/2 teaspoon curry powder
1 large clove garlic, minced
salt and pepper, to taste (remember that Chinese noodles add more salt)
2 whole boneless chicken breasts, quickly poached in chicken broth and cubed
1 cup Chinese noodles
1/2 cup cashew pieces

Mix all ingredients, except noodles and nuts in a bowl; let sit overnight in refrigerator, covered. Flavor of seasonings usually intensifies overnight. Add additional lemon juice, garlic and curry powder, to taste. Before serving, add Chinese noodles and cashews; toss. If not salty enough, add a little more salt.

Meredith's Scala Chopped Salad

Yield: Serves 4 entrée or 8 side salads

SALAD
2 packages mixed escarole, endive and radicchio
1 15 ounce can garbanzo beans
1 teaspoon cracked black pepper
1 cup shredded soy mozzarella
1 cup chopped dry Italian salami
1 cup chopped turkey breast
4 to 8 pepperoncinis, garnish

DRESSING
1 tablespoon fresh lemon juice
1 tablespoon lemon pepper
3 tablespoons red wine vinaigrette

Combine all salad ingredients and toss with dressing. Leave out meats for vegetarians or if using real cheese.

Susan's Basic Vinaigrette

1/2 teaspoon garlic powder
1 teaspoon Dijon mustard
2 teaspoons dried dill
1/4 teaspoon pepper
1/4 cup olive oil
6 tablespoons rice wine vinegar or a combination of balsamic and rice vinegar, or a combination of lemon juice and vinegar

Whisk all ingredients in a bowl. Store in a glass jar in the refrigerator.

Cucumber Salad

1 quart white vinegar
1 cup sugar
3 tablespoons salt
1 teaspoon celery seed
1 1/2 pounds pickling cucumbers, sliced
1 red bell pepper, sliced
1 green bell pepper, sliced
1 large onion, sliced

Boil white vinegar, sugar, and salt; cool slightly; add celery seed. Pour liquid mixture over sliced vegetables. Refrigerate overnight.

Note: If you only have 1 day, slice cucumbers thinner. If you serve another salad, this is enough for about 25.

Fish

Fish

Gefilte Fish by Eda

8 pounds fresh fish: 3 pounds white fish, 2 pounds carp, 2 pounds pike, 1 pound sucker
1 large carrot per pound of fish (8 carrots), sliced
1 large onion per pound of fish (8 onions), sliced
1 stalk celery per pound of fish (8 stalks of celery), sliced
8 eggs
matzo meal, to bond mixture
salt and pepper, to taste

Have market grind fish and give you heads and skin for broth. Layer heads and skin in large rectangular pan. Place sliced onions, carrots and celery on top of heads and skin. Cover with water. Bring to a boil and let simmer. Mix ground fish in large bowl. Discard heads and skin from broth; reserve broth. Use food processor to chop carrots, onions and celery from broth. Beat eggs in food processor. Add mixture of vegetables and eggs to fish. Use food processor to blend and add matzo meal to thicken. Spoon 3 to 4 ounces in oval shape or round shape. Add to boiling broth. Layer fish and cook approximately 1 hour. Remove fish and pour some broth over fish, it will jell.

Karen's Gefilte Fish Mold

Yield: Serves 10

1 carrot, sliced
6 pounds white fish (boned, skinned, ground 2x), net weight 3 to 3 1/2 pounds
2 large onions, ground fine
3 large carrots, ground fine
1/2 cup matzo meal
1 1/2 teaspoons salt
1/2 cup sugar

Spray Bundt pan with nonstick spray. Arrange sliced carrot on bottom of Bundt pan (this is used as a decoration). Mix rest of ingredients. Pack together into Bundt pan. Bake at 350 degrees for 1 hour. As soon as the fish is ready, flip fish out of pan onto a tray and cover with plastic wrap. Place in refrigerator immediately (heat and wrap makes jelly).

Tip: Can be make 1 day ahead. Slice when ready to use.

Ceviche

Yield: Serves 6-7 as an appetizer

Ceviche, a raw fish dish, said to have been created by the Indians of South and Central America, found its way north with the Spaniards. Ceviche is remarkable in that the fish is cooked, not by placing it over or under a heat source, but by marinating it in lemon juice. The fish develops a very interesting texture and no one will suspect that the fish was not literally cooked!

1 pound firm-fleshed white-meat fish fillets (halibut, cod, sole, etc.)
juice of 3 or 4 lemons, enough to cover the fish completely
1 medium-sized onion, finely chopped
1 large or 2 medium-sized tomatoes, cubed
a few coriander leaves, cut into small pieces
1/4 cup pimento-stuffed small olives, optional
1/4 cup olive oil
7/8 cup ketchup
1 medium-sized avocado, cut into small squares, optional
salt to taste
lettuce leaves
1 lime, garnish, optional

Wash fish and cut into uniformly small squares. Place in a 2 to 3 inch deep dish; cover with lemon juice. Refrigerate and let marinate overnight. When "cooked," the fish will appear to be a deeper white. Strain off about 2/3 of lemon juice. Add remaining ingredients, except lettuce leaves and lime. Gently toss to mix well. Cover and refrigerate for at least 1 hour to blend flavors. To serve, with a slotted spoon, remove fish and vegetables from marinade. Place atop lettuce leaves or into individual coupe dishes. If you like, spoon some marinade over each serving. A delicious fish course, or serve atop rice for a main course. A standing slice of lime atop each coupe serving of ceviche makes a lovely garnish. To prepare, slice a lime thinly. Cut through rind and through center of slice 3/4 to other side. Then twist slice so it will stand up.

Crunchy Fish Nuggets with Lemon Tartar Sauce

Yield: Serves 4

Preheat oven to 450 degrees

1 pound skinless halibut fillets or other white fish
1 egg, or egg substitute equivalent
2 tablespoons skim milk
1/4 cup grated Parmesan cheese
1/4 cup cornflake crumbs or plain dry bread crumbs
1/2 teaspoon paprika

Rinse fish and pat dry. Cut fish into 24 bite-size pieces. Set aside. In a medium bowl, combine egg or egg substitute and skim milk. In a large plastic bag with a tight-fitting seal, combine Parmesan cheese, crumbs and paprika. Add fish chunks to egg mixture, stirring until well coated. Using a slotted spoon, remove fish from egg mixture and place several in bag with crumb mixture. Seal bag and toss until fish is well coated with crumbs. Repeat until all fish is coated. Arrange fish in a single layer on a baking sheet or a shallow baking pan. Bake about 5 minutes, or until fish flakes easily with a fork. Serve fish with tartar sauce.

TARTAR SAUCE

1/2 cup mayonnaise
2 tablespoons dill pickle, finely chopped
1 teaspoon lemon rind, finely shredded
1 teaspoon lemon juice
salt and pepper

In a small bowl mix first 4 ingredients together. Add salt and pepper to taste.

Fish with Almonds

14 tablespoons butter or margarine, divided
8 tablespoons sliced almonds, divided
2 1/2 pounds fish of your choice
1 tablespoon lemon juice
1 tablespoon parsley, chopped

In frying pan, melt 2 tablespoons butter; add 4 tablespoons almonds. Stir until golden brown, set aside. In same pan, melt remaining butter over medium heat, add fish. Cook until lightly brown on both sides (about 5 minutes on each side), add more butter if needed. When fish is cooked, sprinkle almonds on fish, then sprinkle lemon juice and parsley. Remove with wide spatula.

Roasted Halibut and Cauliflower Pancake with Hibiscus Chipotle Glaze

Yield: Serves 4

PANCAKES

1 cup cauliflower
2 whole eggs
1/2 cup matzo meal
kosher salt
butter or margarine, for frying

Steam cauliflower until tender. Purée with eggs, matzo meal and salt. Place butter or margarine in a frying pan on medium heat. Ladle 3-inch round batter into pan and fry pancakes on both sides. Set aside.

HIBISCUS CHIPTOLE GLAZE

1/4 cup hibiscus flowers (found in tea section of supermarkets)
1/2 cup sugar
1 tablespoon pure chipotle pepper (smoked jalapeño pepper)
  or pure jalapeño pepper, chopped
2 cups water
1 orange peel, zested
kosher salt, to taste

In a saucepan, add all ingredients and heat, reducing to 3/4 cup. Blend all ingredients and strain through a colander. Check seasoning and keep warm.

ROASTED HALIBUT

4 six ounce halibut fillets

Sear halibut fillets until golden brown and cooked through. To serve, place 1 pancake on each plate and drizzle with Hibiscus Chipotle Glaze. Place 1 halibut fillet beside pancake.

Pan-Seared Tuna with Mandarin Orange Pico De Gallo

Yield: Serves 4

vegetable cooking spray
1/2 cup onion, chopped
1 teaspoon minced garlic
1 tablespoon balsamic vinegar or red wine vinegar
1 teaspoon brown sugar, firmly packed
1/8 teaspoon red pepper flakes, crushed
1 11 ounce can Mandarin orange sections, drained
1/3 cup chopped tomato
1/3 cup chopped avocado
1 tablespoon lime juice
2 tuna steaks (1/2 pound each)
wild rice, optional

Spray a medium saucepan with vegetable cooking spray. Add onion and garlic; cook over medium-high heat until onion is tender, about 5 minutes. Stir in vinegar, brown sugar and pepper flakes. Cook and stir until the sugar dissolves, 2 to 3 minutes. Remove from heat and stir in the remaining ingredients, except tuna and wild rice. Set aside. Rinse fish and pat dry. Set aside. Spray a large skillet. Place over medium-high heat. When skillet is hot, put tuna in and cook about 5 minutes per side, or until fish flakes easily when tested with a fork. Cut each steak in half to make 4 portions. Serve fish with Mandarin orange mixture (and wild rice, optional).

Mango Chutney Chilean Sea Bass

1 pound Chilean sea bass
2 tablespoons lite soy sauce
2 tablespoons lemon juice
2 tablespoons mango chutney

Cut sea bass into individual serving pieces. Place in a baking casserole. Sprinkle with soy sauce and lemon juice. Place about 1 teaspoon of chutney on top of each piece of fish. Bake until done, about 30 minutes, at 350 degrees.

Pan Seared Sea Bass with Swiss Chard

Yield: Serves 4

1 medium Spanish onion, sliced
vegetable or olive oil
1 bunch Swiss chard, coarsely chopped
4 6 ounce sea bass fillets
salt and pepper, to taste
3 golden tomatoes

Sauté onion in olive oil over low-heat; cooking slowly until golden brown (about 30 minutes). When fully caramelized, add Swiss chard; remove from heat; reserve. In second pan, heat small amount of oil, season sea bass with salt and pepper; sear. Turn, reduce heat and finish cooking. On a separate tray, roast tomatoes in oven until done, remove, purée and strain. On center of plate, place Swiss chard and onion mixture, sea bass on top; pour puréed sauce over fish.

Sole Provençal

2 pounds tomatoes, chopped
4 cloves garlic, pressed
2 tablespoons capers, drained
1/2 cup thinly sliced fresh basil leaves or 4 tablespoons, dried
4 tablespoons olive oil, divided
salt and pepper, to taste
1 1/2 pounds sole, tilapia or halibut fillets
1/2 cup white or whole-wheat flour

Combine tomatoes, garlic, capers, basil, 2 tablespoons olive oil, 1/4 teaspoon salt and 1/4 teaspoon pepper in bowl; set aside. Preheat oven to 400 degrees. Rinse fish and pat dry. Lightly sprinkle with salt and pepper; dredge in flour. Heat large skillet; add 1 tablespoon olive oil. Add several fillets to pan and cook 1 minute on each side; then remove to ovenproof dish. Add oil and repeat with remaining fillets. Place fish in single layer in ovenproof dish, spread tomato mixture over top; bake until fish flakes with fork, 5 to 7 minutes. Serve with rice.

Salmon with Barbecue Sauce

Yield: Serves 4

1/2 cup thick and spicy barbecue sauce
1 3/4 tablespoons brown sugar
4 salmon fillets (1 pound)

Mix barbecue sauce and brown sugar until well blended; set aside. Place salmon on rack of broiler pan 3 to 5 inches from heat; broil 4 minutes on each side. Brush generously with barbecue sauce mixture. Broil an additional 2 to 4 minutes or until salmon flakes easily with fork. Turn once and brush occasionally with remaining barbecue sauce mixture. Serve with hot cooked rice.

Salmon with Dijon Mustard

2 salmon steaks
2 tablespoons Dijon mustard
2 tablespoons lite soy sauce
2 tablespoons lemon juice

Place salmon steaks in a casserole that can be used in the broiler. Spread mustard thinly on fish. Sprinkle fish with soy sauce and lemon juice. Broil until done, about 15 minutes, depending on thickness of fish. No need to turn fish, just broil on 1 side.

Salmon à la Sol

1 pound fresh salmon, not too thick
3 teaspoons olive oil
10 to 12 whole garlic cloves
1 1/2 tablespoons hoisin sauce

Rinse the fish, pat dry. Cut into 2 to 3 equal servings, while you heat skillet using olive oil. Add garlic cloves and sauté until starting to turn golden brown (about 7 to 10 minutes). Add fish to skillet and cover with hoisin sauce. Cook approximately 5 minutes until golden brown, then turn. Cook another 5 minutes.

Serve over garlic mashed potatoes with sautéed asparagus.

Salmon Cucumber Chili Salad

Yield: Serves 4
Prep and Cooking Time: 20 Minutes

This is a refreshing salmon salad. The combination of flavors gives you a delicious way of enjoying the healthy benefits of salmon and cucumbers. Using our stovetop cooking method for the salmon, with no oils, makes this especially healthy and light.

3 cups chopped cucumber, washed and unpeeled
2 teaspoons chopped jalapeno pepper, seeds and stems removed (or to taste)
1/2 cup chopped scallions
3 tablespoons chopped fresh mint
1 1/2 pounds salmon fillet, skin removed, cut into 4 pieces
3 tablespoons fresh lemon juice, divided
salt and cracked black pepper, to taste
1 tablespoon soy sauce
1 tablespoon extra virgin olive oil
minced chili pepper, optional
cilantro sprigs

Mix first 4 ingredients together. Preheat a stainless steel 10- to 12-inch skillet, on medium-high heat, for 2 minutes. Rub salmon with 2 tablespoons lemon juice; season with a little salt and pepper. Place salmon in hot pan and cook for 2 to 3 minutes. Turn and cook another 2 to 3 minutes, depending on thickness of salmon. It is best to check salmon for doneness about 1 minute after you have turned it. Salmon is best cooked medium. Insert tip of a knife into thickest part of fillet. It should flake, yet still be pink in center. While salmon is cooking, finish chopping ingredients; whisk together lemon juice, soy sauce, olive oil, salt and pepper. You may want to add pepper a little at a time, so it will match your personal preference in spiciness. When ready to serve, toss with cucumber mixture. Do not toss ahead, as it will dilute the flavor. Place cucumber salad on a platter and place salmon on top. Garnish with a sprig of cilantro and serve.

Maple Glazed Salmon

2 pounds whole salmon fillet
1/3 cup top quality pure Grade B Maple Syrup
(Grade B is dark amber in color and has a richer maple flavor.)
1 tablespoon Dijon mustard
1 teaspoon honey
1 tablespoon cider vinegar
1 tablespoon soy sauce

Place salmon in 9x13 glass dish. Mix sauce ingredients together and pour over salmon. Bake at 375 degrees for 18 minutes. When making 2 fillets of salmon, put them side by side in a large aluminum foil baking pan and double the sauce recipe.

Freezes well.

Poached Salmon with Dijon Dill Sauce

FISH
1 8 ounce salmon fillet

POACHING LIQUID
1 1/2 cups water
1 1/2 cups white wine
1 carrot, diced
1 onion, diced
1 stalk celery, diced

Poaching salmon: Combine ingredients for poaching liquid in saucepan. Bring to boil and reduce to simmer. Place salmon in liquid and poach for 8 to 10 minutes, depending on thickness (8 minutes per inch thick).

DIJON DILL SAUCE
1 teaspoon shallots, minced
1 teaspoon garlic, minced
1 tablespoon butter
1 teaspoon fresh or dry dill weed
1 teaspoon Dijon mustard
1 cup heavy cream
sprigs of dill, garnish
lemon wedges, garnish

Sauce: Sauté shallots and garlic in butter until tender. Add dill, Dijon mustard and heavy cream. Bring to boil and reduce liquid to sauce consistency. Place salmon on a plate, cover with sauce, garnish with a sprig of dill and lemon wedges.

Salmon Loaf for Home and Temple

1 16 ounce can red salmon
2 extra-large eggs
3/4 to 1 cup milk
3/4 to 1 cup seasoned Italian bread crumbs (add a little extra if loose)
1/2 large onion
finely grated carrots for extra color
garlic powder, to taste

Remove bones and mash fish finely. Add and mix together remaining ingredients. Form into loaf and place in loaf pan. Bake at 350 degrees for 45 minutes.

Salmon En Papillote with French Green Beans, Parsley and Garlic

Yield: Serves 1, increase ingredients for as many servings as you wish to make.

1 ounce green beans
kosher salt
fresh lemon juice
3 ounce salmon fillet
equal parts minced garlic, parsley, salt and pepper
toasted almond pieces

Preheat oven to 400 degrees. Tear aluminum foil or parchment to a large enough size to fold in half and provide 4 inch overlap at least on each side. This will provide enough space to create packet. At bottom third of aluminum foil or parchment paper, place green beans; sprinkle with salt and lemon juice to taste. Place salmon fillet on top of green beans and sprinkle with lemon juice. Spread a liberal layer of parsley mixture on top of salmon and a smattering of almonds. Fold aluminum foil or parchment over assembled salmon and continue making packet by folding each of 3 sides until it is sealed. Bake in oven on a sheet pan for 14 minutes. To serve, slide packet onto a plate and slit the top with a knife. Be careful, as steam will escape.

Roasted Salmon

Yield: Serves 4-6

1 6 ounce can pineapple juice
2 tablespoons lemon juice
1 24 ounce salmon fillet
2 tablespoons brown sugar
4 teaspoons chili powder
2 teaspoons lemon peel, grated
3/4 teaspoon ground cumin
1/2 teaspoon salt
1/4 teaspoon ground cinnamon

Combine juices in large zipper bag and marinate salmon in bag for 1 hour, turning a few times. Discard marinade. Combine sugar, chili powder, lemon peel, ground cumin, salt and cinnamon in a bowl, rub over fish. Place on a foil-lined jelly-roll pan that has been sprayed with cooking spray. Cook in a preheated 400 degree oven for 12 minutes or until fish flakes easily. Creates a brown caramelized crust that keeps the fish moist.

Roasted Salmon with Figs in a Wine Sauce

Yield: Serves 4-6
Prep: Preheat oven to 450 degrees

3 tablespoons olive oil, divided
1 pound yellow onions, halved and thinly sliced, to measure 4 cups
salt, to taste
1 cup (6 ounces) dried or fresh figs, stemmed and halved
1/2 cup red or white wine
1/2 cup pareve chicken or vegetable broth
1 tablespoon balsamic vinegar
1 tablespoon chopped fresh rosemary or 1 teaspoon dried rosemary
freshly ground black pepper, to taste
1 1/3 pounds salmon fillet, skinned and cut into 4 portions
parsley, chopped

Swirl 2 tablespoons olive oil in bottom of medium nonstick skillet. Add onions and sprinkle with 1/2 teaspoon salt. Cover and cook over medium-low heat, stirring occasionally, until onions are soft, about 10 minutes. Remove cover and cook, stirring often, until onions are golden, 15 to 20 minutes. Stir in figs, wine, broth, vinegar and rosemary. Increase heat to high; when boiling, lower to simmer until sauce thickens, about 5 minutes. Add salt and pepper, to taste. Keep warm.

Sprinkle salmon with salt and pepper, to taste. Place the fillets on lightly oiled (1 tablespoon) heavy baking sheet. Roast for 7 to 10 minutes or until fish flakes. Sprinkle salmon with parsley. Serve over fig sauce.

Salmon Stuffed with Spinach and Goat Cheese

This recipe is delicious any time of the year. It is especially so around the third or fourth day of Passover, when we are all so full of brisket, chicken and matzo!

1 3 to 4 pound salmon
3 pounds fresh spinach or 2 10 ounce packages frozen, chopped spinach
3 tablespoons margarine
1/4 cup shallots or onions, chopped
1/2 cup chopped fresh basil (substitute 2 tablespoons dried)
1/4 cup chopped fresh chives or green onion tops
4 ounces goat cheese
1/3 cup low-fat sour cream
salt and white pepper
1 1/2 cups dry white wine
2 tablespoons lemon juice
lemon slices, basil and parsley for garnish

FISH
A 4 pound salmon will serve about 8 people. Use 1 whole or center-cut piece of salmon, approximately 4 pounds. Have fishmonger "butterfly" fish and remove center bone. Wipe inside and outside of fish with paper towels and remove any obvious small bones.

STUFFING
Remove stems and wash 3 pounds of fresh, bulk spinach and cook in a small amount of water until soft (approximately 2 minutes). Drain well, squeeze out water using paper towel or an old hand towel. Chop spinach. (Frozen, chopped spinach is much faster and easier to deal with.) Melt margarine. Sauté shallots or onions until soft. Stir in spinach. Remove pan from heat. Stir in basil. Add chives or green onions, goat cheese, sour cream, salt and white pepper, to taste. Mix well and cool to room temperature. This may be covered and refrigerated overnight.

PREPARING FISH
Spray a large shallow ovenproof glass dish or roasting pan (big enough to hold the fish) with nonstick cooking spray. Line pan with a doubled layer of aluminum foil, extending beyond dish, so you can fold it up to hold in juices. Spray aluminum foil as well. Stuff fish with spinach stuffing, spreading it inside salmon. Salmon can be refrigerated at this point for up to 8 hours. Bring it to room temperature before cooking. Preheat oven to 350 degrees. Pour white wine plus lemon juice over salmon in dish. Wrap extended pieces of aluminum foil around fish so that it holds in juice. Cover tightly with additional aluminum foil or a heavy lid. Bake until fish looks opaque (no bright pink left) when flaked with tip of a knife. Fish that is 3 inches high in middle will take approximately 1 hour to cook. Add 10 to 12 minutes for each additional inch of fish, when measured in middle. Remove fish from pan. Discard juice. Carefully open aluminum foil. It will be hot and steamy. Scrape off skin from fish with a sharp knife. Turn over and scrape skin off other side of fish, unless skin has been previously removed. Place fish on large platter and garnish with lemon slices, basil leaves and parsley. Serve hot, warm or at room temperature. Fish can be cooked previous day, brought to room temperature 2 hours before serving and warmed or served at room temperature.

Salmon with Tomatoes and Capers

Yield: Serves 4
Prep: 12 minutes

1 cup chopped yellow onion
1 cup chopped fennel
3 tablespoons olive oil, divided
2 teaspoons minced garlic
28 ounces canned plum tomatoes, drained
1 teaspoon kosher salt
3/4 teaspoon freshly ground black pepper
2 tablespoons vegetable broth
1/2 tablespoon dry white wine
1/2 cup chopped fresh basil leaves
2 tablespoons capers, drained
1 tablespoon butter
4 1 inch thick salmon fillets (abut 2 1/2 pounds)
fresh basil leaves

For the sauce, cook onions and fennel in 2 tablespoons olive oil in a large sauté pan on medium-low heat for 10 minutes, until vegetables are soft. Add garlic and cook for 30 seconds. Add drained tomatoes, smashing them in pan with fork, plus salt and pepper. Simmer on low heat for 15 minutes. Add vegetable broth and white wine; simmer for 10 more minutes to reduce liquid. Add basil, capers, butter; cook for 1 minute more. Prepare a grill with hot coals. Brush salmon with 1 tablespoon olive oil; sprinkle with salt and pepper. Grill on high heat for 5 minutes on each side, until center is no longer raw. Do not overcook. Place sauce on the bottom of a plate, arrange salmon on top and garnish with basil leaves. Serve hot or at room temperature.

Salmon Trifle

Yield: Serves 12

SALAD

2 pounds fresh salmon fillets
2 pounds small red potatoes
1 red pepper
1 yellow pepper
2 medium purple onions
7 pickling cucumbers

DRESSING

1 cup olive oil (not extra-virgin)
2 cloves fresh garlic
1/2 cup plus 1 tablespoon balsamic vinegar
1/4 cup light brown sugar, packed
1 teaspoon coarse kosher salt
1/4 cup freshly grated Parmesan cheese
6 basil leaves, no stems

To make salad, broil salmon until well done on both sides. Leave skin on until ready to assemble salad. Cover and refrigerate. Boil potatoes whole until slightly soft, approximately 20 minutes. Cool and refrigerate. Slice peppers and onions lengthwise, then into thin half-circles. Separate onion slices. Toss peppers and onions in a bowl with 3 tablespoons of dressing. Cover and refrigerate.

To make dressing, place oil and garlic in a blender; pulse. Add remaining dressing ingredients and pulse several times until basil is just chopped. Cover and refrigerate.

To assemble salad, slice cucumbers and potatoes into thin rounds and set aside. Remove skin from salmon and break into bite-sized pieces. Drain peppers and onions; discard marinade. Line bottom of a glass bowl and a little up the sides with 1/2 of cucumber rounds. Next, layer 1/2 of drained onions and peppers. Follow with a layer of potatoes, then half of salmon. Drizzle with 1/2 of dressing. Layer with remaining potatoes, then with onions and peppers (save some for garnish). Layer remaining salmon on top. Tuck cucumbers completely around edge of salad with cut sides showing through bowl. Garnish top of salad with remaining peppers, onions and cucumbers. Drizzle rest of dressing over top. DO NOT TOSS. Serve with a slotted spoon.

Meat

Meat

Turkish Borekes

1 pound filo dough
1 pound ground meat
2 onions (large or small)
1 egg
white of another egg, to seal the Borekes
1 bunch fresh parsley, chopped
salt, to taste
pepper, to taste
vegetable oil

Mix all ingredients (except filo) and sauté, until there is no red in the meat. Remove excess grease. Set pan off heat and let mixture cool. Heat oil (3/4 to 1 inch deep) in another fry pan. Cut filo into wedges (like a slice of pie). Spoon some mixture onto filo wedge and roll up, dip end point into beaten egg white. Place into hot oil only a few minutes; until it turns golden. Remove with tongs and drain each end.

Hint: While working with filo, keep a damp (not wet) towel over unused portion. Otherwise it will dry out very quickly. Best fried in deep fryer and served immediately.

Cabbage and Meatballs

1 pound ground beef
1/2 cup bread crumbs
1 egg
1 large can tomato-vegetable juice, divided
onion powder
seasoned salt, to taste
1 head cabbage
1 tablespoon lemon juice
1/2 cup beef bouillon
1/2 cup sugar
1 10 ounce package frozen baby peas

Combine ground beef, bread crumbs, egg, 1 cup tomato-vegetable juice, onion powder and seasoned salt. Chop cabbage to desired size; put in pot along with remaining tomato-vegetable juice, 1 tablespoon lemon juice, beef bouillon and sugar, simmer until soft. Shape meatballs and put under cabbage; simmer for about 1 hour. Steam peas 5 minutes before serving; put on top of meal when served.

Oriental Meat Balls

Yield: Serves 4

MEAT BALLS

1 large egg
1/4 teaspoon ground ginger
2 tablespoons flour
1 pound ground beef
monosodium glutamate (MSG), to taste
garlic powder, to taste
salt, to taste
vegetable oil

Combine egg, ginger and flour. Mix well to form a smooth batter. Blend ground beef, MSG, garlic powder and salt. Form into walnut-sized balls. Heat some oil in a large frying pan. Dip meat balls into egg batter. Place in heated oil; brown on all sides.

SAUCE

1/2 cup sugar
2 tablespoons vinegar
2 tablespoons soy sauce
1/8 teaspoon ginger
2 teaspoons cornstarch
1/2 cup pineapple chunks
1/2 cup pineapple syrup

Blend above ingredients for sauce, stirring constantly. Place fried meat balls into a casserole dish. Pour sauce over them. Heat at 350 degrees for 45 minutes.

Variation: Serve over cooked spinach. Serve with fried rice or use as hors d'oeuvre with toothpicks.

Sweet and Sour Meatballs

4 pounds ground beef
2 eggs
1/2 cup bread crumbs
1/2 teaspoon garlic powder
salt and pepper, to taste

Mix all ingredients together. Form into tiny balls.

SAUCE

1 jar grape jelly
1 bottle chili sauce
2 cups water
1 can cranberry sauce
1 1/2 tablespoons lemon juice

In large Dutch oven, mix all ingredients and bring to boil. Add meatballs and simmer for 1 hour.

Variation: Add layers of sliced onion and cabbage between each meatball addition.

Barbecued Short Ribs

2 pounds short ribs, cut in 2 inch pieces
1/4 cup minced onions
1/4 cup ketchup
1/4 cup water
2 tablespoons fresh lemon juice
1 tablespoon mustard
salt, to taste
2 tablespoons brown sugar
1 tablespoon Worcestershire sauce

Trim top layer of fat from short ribs. Place several pieces of fat in a Dutch oven and cook over medium heat until bottom is lightly coated with fat. Brown short ribs on all sides; remove when they are done. Add onion and sauté slightly until lightly browned. Return short ribs to pot; add ketchup, water, lemon juice, mustard, salt, brown sugar and Worcestershire sauce. Cover pot and cook over low heat for 2 hours or until tender, stirring occasionally.

Noelle's Barbeque Short Ribs

Yield: Serves 4-6

4 to 5 pounds beef flanken (short ribs) with and without bones
2 tablespoons chili powder
1 tablespoon cumin
1/8 to 1/4 teaspoon cayenne (red pepper)
4 cloves fresh garlic, minced
2 cups barbeque sauce
1/2 cup dry red wine, divided

In a small bowl, mix together dry spices until combined. Using a canning jar, or a container large enough to shake and mix 3 cups, pour in barbeque sauce. Add spice mixture, garlic and 1/4 cup wine. Cover tightly and shake until all ingredients are combined. Using 1 or 2 zipper gallon plastic bags, pour in 1/3 to 1/2 sauce. Add meat, turning to coat pieces. Add remaining sauce to fully cover pieces. Using remaining 1/4 cup red wine, pour wine into mixing container to loosen spices and sauce stuck to sides. Shake well; add to bags. Marinate for 6 hours or overnight. Turn often to distribute marinade. Preheat oven to 450 degrees. Line roaster pan with aluminum foil. Transfer meat to a large roaster, taking as little marinade as possible. Reserve marinade; store in refrigerator. Bake meat, uncovered, for 30 minutes, turning once in middle. Remove meat from oven, pour off fat. Remove bag of marinade. Snip one corner of bag and squeeze out remaining sauce over meat, distributing well. Reduce oven to 350 degrees; cover meat with aluminum foil. Bake for 2 to 3 hours, until meat is tender. Remove meat and serve with sauce on the side.

Note: Increase amount of meat if only meat with bones is used. The bones give it a little more flavor.

Braised Short Ribs with Chocolate and Rosemary

Yield: Serves 6-8

canola or canola-blend oil
6 pounds bone-in short ribs (6 to 7 pounds if using boneless ribs)
salt and pepper
1 1/2 cups finely chopped onions
1/4 cup finely chopped shallots
1/4 cup finely chopped celery
1/4 cup finely peeled and chopped carrots
3 garlic cloves, minced
2 cups dry red wine
3 cups low-salt broth
2 cups canned diced tomatoes, chopped, drained
2 tablespoons chopped fresh parsley
1 very large fresh thyme sprig
1 bay leaf
3 tablespoons shaved or grated bittersweet chocolate
2 tablespoons unsweetened cocoa powder (preferably Dutch process)
1 teaspoon finely chopped fresh rosemary

Heat enough oil to cover bottom of a heavy large pot. Sprinkle ribs with salt and pepper. Working in batches, brown ribs in pot over medium-high heat, until brown on all sides, about 8 minutes per batch. Transfer to plate. Add onions and next 4 ingredients to pot. Cover, reduce heat to medium; cook until vegetables are soft, stirring occasionally, about 10 minutes. Add wine. Boil uncovered, until liquid is reduced by half, scraping up browned bits, about 5 minutes. Add broth, tomatoes, parsley, thyme and bay leaf. Return ribs to pot, cover partially and simmer 1 1/2 hours. Uncover and simmer until rib meat is tender, stirring occasionally, about 1 1/2 hours longer. Transfer ribs to plate; discard bay leaf. Spoon fat from surface of sauce. Boil sauce until beginning to thicken, about 8 minutes. Reduce heat to medium. Add chocolate, cocoa powder and rosemary; stir until chocolate melts. Season to taste with salt and pepper. Return ribs to pot. Simmer to rewarm, about 5 minutes.

Hint: Use a good red wine, as it adds depth to the flavors with the chocolate.
Serve with noodles, rice or mashed potatoes.

Ruthie's Flanken Couscous

2 flanken, any size
1 onion, cut in quarters
1 small bag baby carrots
1 cabbage, cut in quarters
1 big piece of banana squash, cut into large pieces
1 can garbanzo beans
3 tablespoons chicken bouillon
1 teaspoon turmeric
1 box couscous
soup broth (chicken or beef)

Put flanken, onion, carrots, cabbage, banana squash and garbanzo beans in big pot. Cover with water; boil until tender. Season with chicken bouillon and turmeric. Take out flanken and vegetables; set aside. Cook couscous in soup broth as directed on box. To serve: Put couscous on bottom of large plate or bowl; place flanken and vegetables on top

Barbara's Pot Roast

4 pounds chuck, cut into 3-inch pieces
flour
salt and pepper, to taste
chicken fat (schmaltz), olive oil can be substituted
2 to 3 onions, cut up
1 8 ounce can tomato sauce
2 bay leaves
parsley
garlic
paprika

Dip meat in mixture of flour, salt and pepper. Sauté in chicken fat, until brown on outside. In large sauce pot, sauté onions until soft and lightly brown. Transfer meat from sauté pan to sauce pot. Add boiling water to cover meat; add tomato sauce. Add spices. Cover and simmer slowly until meat is tender.

Most Delicious Beef Stew

2 pounds beef stew, cut into 1-inch chunks
1 cup Italian dressing
1 large onion, chopped
16 ounces beef broth, divided
3 cups carrots, cut into chunks
3 to 4 medium potatoes, cut into chunks
1 14 ounce can stewed tomatoes, undrained
1 small can tomato paste
salt and pepper, to taste

Put meat and dressing in container, refrigerate 30 minutes to marinate. Cook onions in half beef broth on medium-high heat in Dutch oven, for about 10 minutes or until softened. Remove meat from marinade and discard marinade. Brown meat. Place meat and remaining broth in Dutch oven and bring to boil, stirring occasionally. Reduce heat to low, cover. Simmer for 1 hour or until meat is fork tender. Add carrots, potatoes, tomatoes and tomato paste to meat, simmer; check for "doneness" after 30 minutes, but continue to cook for an additional 30 minutes or so, until meat is falling apart. Continue to cook uncovered for 15 minutes or until tender and sauce is thickened, stirring occasionally. Season with salt and pepper, to taste. Serve with chunks of crusty bread.

Hint: Can be made ahead to enhance flavor.

Beef Stroganoff

olive oil or pareve margarine
8 ounces mushrooms, sliced
2 medium onions, sliced
2 pounds shoulder steak, sliced in strips
flour for dredging
1/2 cup white wine, plus a little extra for deglazing
2 tablespoons Dijon mustard
2 cups beef stock
1 pint pareve sour cream (find at kosher market), divided
1 tablespoon Worcestershire sauce
salt and pepper to taste
egg noodles or rice, cooked

Melt margarine or heat olive oil and sauté mushrooms. Add onions. In a separate pan, brown strips of meat after dredging in flour. Set aside. When onions and mushrooms are cooked, deglaze both pans with white wine and Dijon mustard. Combine all ingredients into one pan. Add beef stock, 1/2 cup white wine and half of pareve sour cream. Simmer for 30 to 45 minutes, uncovered. Stir well. Just prior to serving, add remainder of pareve sour cream. Stir to combine. Serve over noodles or rice.

Beef Tomato

1 1/2 pounds shoulder chuck, cut into strips across the grain
1/4 cup soy sauce
1/4 cup beef bouillon
4 tablespoons flour
3 tablespoons sugar
2 tablespoons vegetable or olive oil
2 stalks celery, sliced diagonally
1 onion, chopped
1 medium green pepper, sliced or pea pods
4 tomatoes, quartered
salt and pepper, to taste

Put meat in bowl, pour soy sauce and bouillon over meat. Let stand for 15 minutes or longer, if desired. Remove from marinade. Combine flour and sugar. Heat oil in heavy pan, add meat and stir flour/sugar mixture into meat until brown. Pour marinade over meat; stir until liquid thickens. Cover pot and cook briefly, until meat is tender. Add celery, onion, peppers or pea pods and tomatoes, salt and pepper, to taste. Simmer covered about 10 minutes. Serve over rice.

Rose's Chuck Steak

1 chuck steak
1/2 cup barbecue sauce
1/2 cup orange juice

Blend together barbecue sauce and orange juice. Spread on steak, wrap in foil, bake at 350 degrees for 1 1/2 to 2 hours

Summer Steak Salad with Ginger-Lime Dressing

Yield: Serves 4

Known in Asia as Shaking Beef Salad, or bo luc lac, this Vietnamese classic is made by shaking, essentially searing, steak in a very hot pan. Jasmine or brown rice would be ideal alongside. It is also great for using leftover steak or roast; just toss in marinade before reheating.

GINGER-LIME DRESSING

3 tablespoons fish sauce
2 tablespoons sugar
2 tablespoons fresh lime juice
2 tablespoons water or salad oil
1 tablespoon ginger, peeled and minced
2 garlic cloves, minced
1 teaspoon red jalapeño chile, minced

Whisk all ingredients in small bowl to blend. You can use the food processor or blender.

MARINADE FOR STEAK

1 tablespoon medium-dry Sherry
2 tablespoons plus 2 teaspoons Tamari soy sauce
2 garlic cloves, minced
1 teaspoon brown sugar, packed
1 1/4 pounds New York steak, trimmed, cut into 2/3 inch cubes

Mix Sherry, Tamari soy sauce, garlic and brown sugar in medium bowl. Stir in steak. Marinate steak at least 30 minutes up to 2 hours, stirring occasionally.

SALAD

2 cups arugula leaves
3 cups mizuna leaves, torn in half if very large (about 1 1/2 ounces)
2 cups torn Bibb lettuce leaves (about 6 large, lightly packed)
1 cup mixed baby greens
1/2 12 ounce English hothouse cucumber, halved lengthwise, sliced very thinly on diagonal
12 cherry tomatoes
2 tablespoons vegetable oil
1/2 medium size red onion, cut into thin wedges
2 shallots, sliced into thin rounds
1/4 medium pineapple, peeled, cored, halved lengthwise, cut crosswise into 1/3 inch thick slices

Combine salad greens, cucumber and tomatoes in large bowl. Add half of dressing and toss to coat. Arrange greens mixture on large rimmed platter. Heat oil in large nonstick skillet over high heat. Add onion and shallots; sauté 30 seconds. Add beef with marinade. Sauté until beef is brown outside, but still pink inside, about 4 minutes. Add pineapple slices and stir until pineapple is heated through, about 1 minute longer. Place steak mixture in center of platter.

Stuffed Bell Peppers with Ground Beef

6 large bell peppers
4 tablespoons margarine
1 cup chopped onion
2 celery ribs, finely chopped
3 tablespoons finely chopped parsley
2 large cloves garlic, thinly minced
2 pounds lean ground beef
3 cups soft bread crumbs
1 teaspoon seasoned salt
1 teaspoon salt
1 scant teaspoon ground black pepper
3 eggs, slightly beaten
1 8 ounce can tomato sauce or Creole seasoned tomatoes

Remove stems and seeds from bell peppers; set aside. Melt margarine in a large skillet over medium-low heat. Add onions, celery, parsley and garlic. Add ground beef; sauté together until beef is completely cooked and vegetables are lightly browned. Add bread crumbs; season with seasoned salt, salt and pepper. Remove from heat; cool slightly. Work the eggs into mixture. If more moisture is needed, add a little broth. Spoon stuffing into prepared bell peppers and place them in a shallow baking dish. Bake in a preheated 350 degree oven for 30 minutes or until peppers are tender. Spoon tomato sauce or tomatoes over each stuffed pepper, bake 5 minutes longer.

Elisha's Crock Pot Ground Beef

2 pounds ground beef
garlic powder, to taste
oil to sauté
1 14.5 ounce can diced tomatoes
1 14 ounce can artichoke bottoms, cut up
1 can black olives
1 green pepper, cut into chunks
1 large onion, diced
2 tablespoons chopped garlic
salt-free seasoning, to taste

Brown beef and garlic powder in oil in saucepan. Drain and place in crock pot. Add all other ingredients, except salt-free seasoning. Sprinkle salt-free seasoning on top. Cover and cook for several hours.

Edie's Stuffed Cabbage

STUFFING

2 1/2 pounds ground beef
2 eggs
1 1/2 cups rolled oats
1 teaspoon garlic powder
salt and pepper, to taste

MARINADE

1 8 ounce can tomato sauce
8 ounces light brown sugar
1 box raisins, lunch-box size
dash of cinnamon
3 cups water

CABBAGE ROLLS

2 heads of cabbage, partially cored and lightly steamed
2 Spanish onions, sliced
1 28 ounce can crushed tomatoes

Preheat oven to 350 degrees. To make stuffing, mix together ground beef, eggs, rolled oats, garlic powder, salt and pepper. Marinade: combine tomato sauce, brown sugar, raisins, cinnamon and water. Roll meat mixture in cabbage leaves; close cabbage in diaper-fashion. If leaves are not soft enough, drop individual leaves back into hot water for 1 minute. Layer cabbage rolls in a roasting pan. Cover with marinade. On each layer of cabbage rolls, put onion slices and some crushed tomatoes. Shred any leftover cabbage and place on top of layers. Cover tightly with a double layer of heavy duty aluminum foil. Bake 2 1/2 hours at 350 degrees.

Betty's Meat Loaf

MEAT LOAF

- 2/3 cup dry bread crumbs
- 1 cup non-dairy creamer
- 1 1/2 pounds ground beef
- 2 eggs, beaten
- 1/4 cup chopped onion
- 1 teaspoon salt
- 1/2 teaspoon sage
- dash of pepper

PIQUANT SAUCE

- 6 tablespoons brown sugar
- 1/2 cup ketchup
- 1/2 teaspoon nutmeg
- 1 teaspoon dry mustard

Soak bread crumbs in non-dairy creamer, add meat, eggs, onion and seasonings; mix well. Place in two 3x6x2 pans (small loaf pans) and cover with piquant sauce. For piquant sauce, mix all ingredients together. Bake at 350 degrees for 45 minutes.

Sweet and Sour Meat Loaf

MEAT LOAF

- 1 medium onion
- 1 large egg
- 1 8 ounce can tomato sauce
- 1 cup crisped rice cereal
- 2 pounds ground beef

TOPPING

- 1 8 ounce can tomato sauce
- 3 to 4 tablespoons brown sugar
- 1 tablespoon white vinegar
- 1 tablespoon yellow mustard

Blend onion, egg and tomato sauce in blender. Hand mix with crisped rice cereal and ground beef. Mold loaf into 9x13 baking dish. Blend tomato sauce, brown sugar, vinegar and mustard; pour over molded loaf. Bake at 350 degrees for 1 hour.

Variation: Place tomato wedges around loaf to absorb some of sauce.

Beef Lengua Marinated in Vinaigrette (Flo's Pickled Tongue)

Yield: Serves 12

STEP 1

1 beef tongue (about 3 pounds)
1 tablespoon salt
3 to 4 bay leaves
1/2 onion, sliced
2 cloves garlic
2 stalks celery, sliced

Rinse tongue thoroughly. Place in a large pot with water to cover plus 1 inch. Add other ingredients. Bring to a boil over medium heat, skimming off the froth as it rises to top. Reduce heat to low, cover and simmer, until a fork inserted in thickest part goes in without resistance, about 3 hours.

STEP 2

3 cloves garlic, thinly sliced
1/2 cup extra-virgin olive oil
1/4 cup Sherry vinegar
1 tablespoon Dijon mustard
1/2 tablespoon salt
1/2 teaspoon freshly ground black pepper
pinch of sugar
2 hard-cooked eggs, peeled, whites chopped and yolk pushed through a sieve
1/4 cup seeded and minced red bell pepper,
1/2 small onion, minced (about 1/4 cup)
2 tablespoons capers
1 tablespoon pitted and finely chopped Kalamata olives
1/2 teaspoon crumbled dried oregano
1 tablespoon chopped fresh basil leaves
1/4 cup minced fresh parsley leaves
French bread for serving

Transfer meat to a cutting board and let stand until cool enough to handle. Skin comes off easily when hot, but not when cold, so remove skin as soon as possible, remove any small bones and gristle. Cut on diagonal into 1/8-inch-thick slices, cutting toward tip and hump, almost parallel to base. Arrange, overlapping layers, in a large glass baking dish. Lay garlic on top. In a medium-size glass bowl, whisk together oil, vinegar, mustard, salt and black pepper, until thickened. Add sugar, egg whites, bell pepper, onion, capers, olives, oregano, basil and parsley. Stir well to combine and pour evenly over tongue. Cover with plastic wrap and let marinate in refrigerator for at least 6 hours or overnight. Arrange a few slices on salad plates and garnish with egg yolks. Serve French bread on side.

Variation: A 3-pound beef sirloin roast can be used instead of tongue (lengua).

Moroccan Couscous with Lamb

Yield: Serves 8

1/2 cup pareve margarine
4 pounds lean lamb, in 2 inch cubes
2 teaspoons salt
1/2 teaspoon pepper
1/2 teaspoon nutmeg
1/4 teaspoon tumeric
1/4 teaspoon cinnamon
1 1/2 pounds onions, quartered and peeled
4 carrots, peeled, cut into 2 inch pieces
4 tomatoes, peeled, seeded, chopped
3 medium zucchini, halved, cut into 2 inch pieces
1/2 cup raisins
1 cup canned chickpeas, drained
16 ounce box precooked couscous

In large pot, over medium-high heat, melt margarine. Add lamb, salt and spices. Stir until meat is well coated. Add 5 cups of water; heat to boiling. Reduce heat, cover and simmer 1 hour. Add remaining ingredients, except couscous. Cover and cook 30 minutes more. Make couscous according to package directions. To serve, mound couscous in serving dish and top with lamb stew.

Rack of Lamb with Lemon Rosemary Baste

Yield: Serves 2

3 tablespoons lemon juice
2 teaspoons dried rosemary
3 teaspoons dried oregano
1/4 teaspoon black pepper
1 tablespoon vegetable oil (more if needed)
1 medium 8 rib rack of lamb

Preheat oven to 475 degrees. Combine lemon juice, rosemary, oregano and black pepper, to taste, in small bowl. Add oil to heavy skillet and sear lamb over high heat for 3 minutes per side. Coat lamb with sauce. To roast, place lamb rack, fat side up, in a roasting pan and roast in middle of oven; 25 minutes for medium. Transfer to a warm plate; let rest for 10 minutes before serving.

You can test for doneness by touch. Prod lamb – when it has a springy, but firm texture and is moderately juicy, meat is done. More well-done meat will have a firmer feel. Lamb is at its best when it is medium-rare or medium, with an internal temperature of 130 to 140 degrees.

Spiced Braised Lamb with Carrots and Spinach

3 1/2 pounds boneless lamb, trimmed and cut into 2 inch pieces
1 teaspoon black pepper
1 1/2 teaspoons salt, divided
1 to 3 tablespoons olive oil
1 large onion, chopped
1 celery rib, chopped
4 garlic cloves, finely chopped
4 teaspoons ground cumin
2 teaspoons ground coriander
2 cups water, divided
1 14 to 16 ounce can whole tomatoes in juice
6 medium carrots, cut crosswise into 2 1/2 inch pieces
1 pound spinach, coarse stems discarded

Preheat oven to 350 degrees. Pat lamb dry; sprinkle with pepper and 1 teaspoon salt. Heat 1 teaspoon oil in a 10 inch heavy skillet, over moderately high heat until hot but not smoking, then brown lamb in 5 batches, turning occasionally, about 4 minutes per batch. Add more oil as needed. Transfer, as browned, to an ovenproof 6 to 7 quart wide heavy pot.

Pour off all but 1 tablespoon fat from skillet, then cook onion and celery over moderate heat, stirring occasionally, until golden, about 3 minutes. Add garlic, cumin and coriander, stir for 1 minute. Add 1 cup water and deglaze skillet by boiling, stirring and scraping up any brown bits, 1 minute, then pour mixture over lamb in pot.

Pour juice from tomatoes into stew, coarsely chop tomatoes; add to stew along with remaining cup of water and remaining 1/2 teaspoon of salt; bring to boil (liquid should almost cover the meat).

Cover and braise lamb in middle of oven, 1 1/2 hours. Stir in carrots and continue to braise until carrots and lamb are tender, 20 to 30 minutes. Transfer pot to top of stove and, working over moderately high heat, stir in spinach by handfuls to soften. Cook uncovered, stirring occasionally, until spinach is tender, 5 to 8 minutes. Season with salt and pepper.

Brisket

1 brisket
Dijon mustard
2 cups brown sugar
2 cans beer
2 16 ounce jars chili sauce
10 Kosher salt crystals

Cover brisket with Dijon mustard; bake at 350 degrees for 2 hours. Mix remaining ingredients. Cook brisket in mixture 2 more hours. Cool, slice and serve. Can be frozen.

Beer Braised Brisket

Yield: Serves 10-12

1 5 to 7 pounds brisket or London Broil
2 teaspoons seasoned salt
1/2 cup brown sugar, packed
2 tablespoons cider vinegar
1 package onion soup mix
1 cup chili sauce
1 12 ounce can beer

Season brisket with seasoned salt. Rub meat with brown sugar, drizzle with vinegar, rub with onion soup mix, cover with chili sauce and sprinkle with beer. Bake at 325 degrees, uncovered, for 2 hours. Cover and continue cooking until done (1 1/2 to 2 hours). Remove meat from gravy and cool in refrigerator overnight. Skim fat from gravy, add small amount of water to dilute gravy. Slice meat and put in an ovenproof casserole. Cover with gravy and seal with foil. Heat at 325 degrees for 1 hour.

Brisket Con Chipotle

Yield: Serves 6

BRAISED BRISKET WITH TOMATO AND CHIPOTLE

1 to 2 pound brisket
kosher salt, to taste
3 tablespoons olive oil
2 tablespoons chopped garlic
1 onion, chopped
6 plum tomatoes, cut in quarters
1/2 tablespoon cumin
1/2 tablespoon dry oregano
1 bottle red wine
4 cups water
3 tablespoons chipotle pepper purée (available in supermarket)
1 bay leaf

Season brisket with salt. In roasting pan, heat oil until smoky hot; sear brisket well on all sides. Transfer brisket to platter. Lower flame and sauté garlic, onion, tomatoes. Add rest of ingredients in this section. Let mixture cook for 10 minutes; season brisket with tomato mixture. Return brisket to roasting pan. Cover and cook in 350 degree oven for 1 1/2 hours, or until very tender. Cool brisket to room temperature. Slice brisket; reheat in same sauce.

MATZAH TORTILLAS

2 cups matzah cake meal
1 teaspoon salt
1 cup warm water
1 tablespoon olive oil, plus additional olive oil for frying

To make matzah tortillas, mix in a bowl, by hand, all ingredients in this section. With hands, form 1 1/2 inch balls, then roll between plastic wrap to form tortilla shape. Using 2 tablespoons olive oil, preheat non-stick griddle or pan on medium flame. Place matzah tortilla on griddle. Cook on both sides, until nice and soft. Pour additional olive oil into a frying pan. Preheat oil to 300 degrees. Fry tortillas in oil, until crisp.

GARNISH

1 red onion, chopped
1 avocado, cut in slices

Serve 2 matzah tortillas per plate, filled with braised brisket and garnished with onion and 1 slice of avocado.

Fruited Brisket

1/2 pound bag mixed dried fruit
1 small bag prunes
1 bottle Kosher wine
1 large onion, sliced in rings
5 to 10 cloves garlic
4 to 5 pound brisket
1/4 teaspoon each seasoned salt, pepper, onion powder, garlic powder
baby carrots

Marinate dried fruit and prunes in wine overnight.

In bottom of baking pan, place onion and garlic cloves. Place brisket on top and season with spices. Pour marinated fruit and wine over top of brisket; sprinkle baby carrots around perimeter of brisket. Cover with aluminum foil. Bake at 350 degrees for 3 hours or until soft. Baste while cooking and add more wine, if needed. Separate compote to serve alongside brisket. Cool brisket, slice, put back into juice. If planning to serve the following day, remove compote, slice meat, put compote back on to reheat, then separate when served.

Brisket with Portobello Mushrooms and Dried Cranberries

2 1/2 cups dry red Kosher for Passover wine
20 ounces canned Kosher for Passover beef or chicken broth
2 1/2 cups cranberry juice
1/2 cup potato starch
2 1/2 large sliced onions
10 cloves of garlic, chopped
3 1/2 to 4 tablespoons chopped fresh rosemary
salt and pepper
10 pounds flat-cut brisket, trimmed
30 ounces medium portobello mushrooms, dark gills removed, caps thinly sliced
2 1/2 cups (10 ounces) dried cranberries

Preheat oven to 325 degrees. Whisk wine, broth and cranberry juice in a bowl. Add potato starch, adding a little juice to the starch first to moisten it. Pour into a large roasting pan. Mix onion, garlic and rosemary. Sprinkle brisket with salt and pepper and place fat side up in pan. Brown brisket. Spoon wine mixture over brisket and cover with onions, garlic and rosemary. Cover with heavy duty aluminum foil. Bake brisket about 5 hours, basting with pan juices every hour or so. Transfer brisket to plate. Cool until cold; can be frozen at this point. Slice thinly across grain. Arrange slices in sauce. Can be covered and refrigerated two days ahead or frozen. Can be frozen in sauce, or sauce and meat can be frozen separately. Wrap very well. To finish, place mushrooms and cranberries in sauce around brisket, cover pan with foil and bake at 350 degrees, until mushrooms are tender and brisket is hot, about 30 minutes, or longer if brisket is cold.

Poultry

Poultry

Minnie's Chicken Paprikash

1 onion, diced
3 stalks celery, chopped
4 to 5 carrots, diced
vegetable oil
paprika
1 chicken, cut up
salt
pepper
garlic powder
1 chicken bouillon cube
2 cups boiling water
1 to 1 1/2 cups cooked rice

Brown onion, celery and carrots in vegetable oil for 5 minutes in large pot. Sprinkle with paprika for color. Season chicken with salt, pepper, garlic powder and paprika; let sit a few minutes. Dissolve bouillon in 2 cups boiling water; add with chicken to vegetables. Cook about 1 hour. Serve over rice.

Israeli Chicken

1 chicken, cut up
salt
pepper
garlic
paprika
1 cup orange juice
1/4 cup honey
10 kumquats or 4 to 5 oranges, sliced

Season chicken with salt, pepper, garlic powder, paprika. Mix together orange juice and honey, until well blended. Pour over chicken in covered roaster. Top with kumquats or orange slices. Bake for 1 hour at 350 degrees. Remove lid for last 15 minutes.

Chicken Fricassee

2 15 ounce cans tomato sauce
1 onion, finely diced in food processor and juice of onion
1/2 teaspoon basil, dried
1/2 teaspoon thyme, dried
salt and pepper, to taste
1/4 teaspoon garlic powder
1 bay leaf
3 teaspoons chicken consommé powder
1 pound necks and gizzards
2 whole chickens, cut in 8 pieces, skin removed
water

Mix tomato sauce, onion, basil, thyme, salt, pepper and garlic powder in bottom of large (wide) Dutch oven. Add bay leaf. Add chicken consommé powder. Add necks, gizzards, breasts, thighs, legs and wings (layered in that order, so that wings are on top; necks and gizzards are on bottom) to sauce in bottom of pot. Add enough water to cover chicken. Now add meatballs to top of pot. Cover pot; bring to a boil on stovetop, cooking on medium high. Once boiling, pot can be moved to a preheated 400 degree oven. Cook approximately 1 1/2 hours total. Chicken should be very soft; almost falling off bones. Serve with Challah to absorb sauce. Feel free to leave out necks and gizzards if they are not to your family's liking. Ours fight over them. This recipe was created by my mother, Adele, for our Rosh Hashanah celebrations and continues today as a traditional meal for the holidays. It works great for a large crowd and does not require a lot of time and attention.

MEATBALLS

1 pound ground beef or turkey
1/2 onion, grated
1/2 peeled potato, grated on small side of grater
1 egg
1/2 garlic powder
1/2 teaspoon onion powder
salt and pepper, to taste

Mix beef or turkey, onion, potato, egg and seasonings together loosely in a bowl. Make into walnut-sized meatballs; add to pot of chicken. Meatballs can be made ahead of time and frozen on a cookie sheet for 2 hours. Place in a plastic bag and store in freezer until you are ready to add them to fricassee pot. They should be thawed just a little bit.

Chicken with Almonds, Djej bi Looz, Moroccan

Yield: Serves 4

1 tablespoon salt
8 cloves garlic, crushed, divided
1 chicken, quartered
2 tablespoons parsley, chopped
1/2 cup olive oil, divided
1/2 teaspoon pepper, or more to taste
pinch or two of saffron
2 medium onions, chopped
1 to 2 ounces whole almonds, blanched
4 hard-boiled eggs, halved

Make a paste by grinding together salt and half of garlic. Rub chicken parts on all sides with this mixture. Rinse well; pat dry with paper towel. In a mortar, combine remaining garlic with parsley; pound to a paste. Moisten mixture with 1 tablespoon of olive oil; add pepper and saffron. With this mixture rub chicken thoroughly. Cover and refrigerate for about 24 hours. Heat 4 tablespoons oil in a heavy flameproof casserole; sauté onion until just golden. Add chicken; continue to sauté until chicken is golden brown on all sides. Add 2 cups of water, bring to a boil, cover, reduce flame; simmer gently for about 45 minutes, turning chicken several times. Add water, if necessary, to prevent casserole from drying out. Heat 1 tablespoon oil in skillet; fry almonds until golden brown. Drain on paper towel. To serve, spoon almonds over chicken, garnish with hard-boiled eggs; serve hot.

Stuffed Moroccan Chicken

1 whole chicken, cleaned out
salt
pepper
garlic powder
paprika
1/2 cup pareve margarine
2 onions, chopped
1/4 cup raisins
1 package pitted prunes
1 package dried apricots, cut up
1/2 cup par-boiled rice
1 teaspoon cinnamon
few shakes cumin and turmeric for color

Season chicken with salt, pepper, garlic powder, paprika. In pan, sauté onions in margarine. Add remaining ingredients. Add salt if necessary. Let cool. Stuff rice mixture into chicken. Bake at 375 degrees for 1 hour.

Apricot-Glazed Chicken

Yield: Serves 8
Prep Time: 30 minutes active; 9 hours marinating

1/2 cup shallots (2 large), finely chopped
1/4 cup finely chopped, peeled ginger
2 tablespoons vegetable oil
1/2 cup red-wine vinegar
2/3 cup soy sauce
1 cup apricot preserves (12 ounces)
salt and pepper
16 chicken drumsticks (4 1/2 pounds)

Cook shallots and ginger in oil in small heavy saucepan over medium-heat, stirring occasionally, until softened and golden, about 5 minutes. Stir in vinegar; boil until reduced by about half, about 2 minutes. Add soy sauce, preserves and 1/4 teaspoon each of salt and pepper; simmer, uncovered, stirring occasionally for 15 minutes. Pureé sauce in blender until smooth (use caution when blending hot liquids), then cool to room temperature. Divide chicken between 2 large sealable bags and pour marinade over chicken. Seal bags, pressing out excess air; marinate, chill, turning bag over occasionally, at least 8 hours.

Preheat oven to 425 degrees, with rack in middle. Line a 17x12 inch shallow heavy baking pan with 2 slightly overlapping sheets of foil, brush foil with small amount of oil. Arrange chicken (with marinade) in 1 layer in pan. Roast chicken, turning once, until deep brown, cooked through and glazed, about 40 minutes total.

Hint: Chicken can be marinated up to 24 hours. Cooked chicken can be kept warm, loosely covered with foil, in a 250 degree oven.

Shoyu Chicken, A Taste of Hawaii

Yield: Serves 6

4 pounds chicken thighs, bone-in
3/4 cup shoyu (soy sauce)
1/4 cup fresh ginger, grated
1 cup water
1/3 cup brown sugar
3 garlic cloves, smashed
1/2 teaspoon ground pepper
4 to 8 stalks green onion, sliced thinly

Heat shoyu; bring to slow boil in 12-inch diameter, nonstick sauté pan. Stir in ginger, water, brown sugar, garlic and ground pepper. Lower heat to simmer; add chicken thighs. Cook chicken in partially covered pan for 35 to 45 minutes. When chicken is almost finished, take lid off; turn heat up to medium-high. Make sure you turn chicken often, so that it creates a glaze and doesn't burn. When the sauce thickens and chicken is glazed, remove chicken, strain out ginger and garlic from sauce. Serve chicken on a bed of steamed rice. Pour sauce over chicken; sprinkle green onion over entire dish.

Variation: Pineapple juice can be substituted or combined with water. Pineapple slices can also be added to top the finished dish.

Robin's Paella

1 chicken, cut up
olive oil or canola oil
1 onion, diced
3 fresh garlic cloves, minced
1 each red and green pepper, sliced
2 small cans diced tomatoes
pinch saffron
3 to 4 sausages, sliced into 1/4 inch slices (could be chicken or turkey)
1 cup peas
2 cups Arborio rice
3 to 4 cups chicken or vegetable broth

Brown chicken in oil in large paella pan or Dutch oven; put aside. Sauté onions. Add garlic and peppers; continue to sauté. Add diced tomatoes with juice and saffron; simmer. Add chicken, sausages, peas, rice and broth. Cover and cook until rice is soft, about 45 to 60 minutes. Do not stir rice too much.

Spiced Chicken Filo Pie

Yield: Serves 6
Prep Time: Ready in approximately 2 hours, 30 minutes

3/4 cup almonds
2 3/4 teaspoons ground cinnamon, divided
1 teaspoon sugar
1 4 pound chicken, neck and giblets removed, cut into 8 pieces
6 cups chicken broth, fat-skimmed
1 1/2 pounds onion, chopped
1 clove garlic, peeled and chopped
2 teaspoons ground ginger
1 1/2 teaspoons turmeric
1 1/4 teaspoons ground cloves
1 1/4 teaspoons salt, divided
1 1/8 teaspoons pepper, divided
6 eggs
6 tablespoons pareve margarine, melted
1 16 ounce package filo dough, thawed
2 tablespoons confectioners sugar

Place almonds in 10-inch baking pan. Bake in 350 degree regular or convection oven until golden beneath skins, about 10 minutes. Let cool. In a food processor, pulse almonds with 3/4 teaspoon cinnamon and sugar until coarsely chopped (or coarsely chop with a knife). Rinse chicken. In a 5 to 6 quart pot, combine chicken, broth, onion, garlic, ginger, turmeric and cloves. Bring to a boil over medium-high heat; reduce heat, cover and simmer until chicken is tender when pierced, about 45 minutes. Pour chicken mixture through a strainer set over a large bowl; return strained broth to pan. Retain onion mixture from strainer. With your fingers, remove skin from chicken and pull meat from bones; discard skin and bones. Shred chicken into bite sized pieces. Mix chicken and strained onion in a bowl and moisten with about 2 tablespoons broth. Season to taste with 1 teaspoon salt, 1 teaspoon pepper and 1/2 teaspoon cinnamon. Let cool if desired, cover and chill up to 1 day. Bring broth in pan to simmer over medium-high heat; reduce heat to maintain simmer. In a bowl, beat eggs to blend with 1/4 teaspoon salt and 1/8 teaspoon pepper. Add eggs to broth, stir gently until set, 1 to 2 minutes. Pour through strainer into another bowl; reserve broth for other uses. Let eggs cool. Lightly brush inside of a shallow 3 to 3 1/2-quart casserole or baking dish with melted margarine. Place one 13x17 sheet of filo in dish so that it covers bottom and sides of casserole and hangs over edge slightly. Brush sheet lightly with margarine. (Directions continue on next page)

Spiced Chicken Filo Pie (continued)

(As you work with filo, cover sheets you're not using.) Continue to layer and brush margarine on three more sheets. Sprinkle half almond mixture evenly over filo in bottom of casserole, spread chicken mixture over nuts. Cut four sheets of filo in half crosswise to make eight 8 1/2-by 13-inch rectangles. One at a time, brush four half-sheets with margarine; layer them over chicken. Sprinkle remaining half of almond mixture over filo; arrange egg mixture evenly over nuts. Fold in overhanging edges of filo and top with four more margarined half-sheets, tucking any overhanging edges into sides of casserole. Brush top layer with margarine. Bake pie in 375 degree regular or convection oven until top is well browned, 35 to 40 minutes. Mix confectioners sugar with remaining 1 1/2 teaspoons cinnamon and sift evenly over top of pie. Cut warm pie into portions; serve warm or at room temperature.

Variation: Spiced, ground almonds are spread over bottom of the pastry before adding chicken filling flavored with turmeric, ginger and cloves in this variation on the much-loved chicken pie.

Hint: Have chicken cut up at meat market. Pie can be assembled up to 2 hours ahead; wrap airtight and chill.

Chicken Pot Pie

5 tablespoons margarine
5 tablespoons all-purpose flour
2 1/2 cups chicken broth
2 cups cooked chicken or turkey, cubed
1 10 ounce package frozen peas and carrots or mixed vegetables
2 small potatoes, cut in cubes (divide cubed potatoes into 4 portions, using 1 portion per pie)
4 unbaked 9 inch pastry shells for individual use (1 for each)

Preheat oven to 350 degrees. In 1-quart saucepan melt margarine. Stir in flour and cook until thick. Blend chicken broth; cook until consistency of gravy.

In order, layer chicken broth, chicken, vegetables and potatoes. Use 4 ovenproof bowls. Cover each bowl with pastry shell pressing at edges to seal. Pastry shell should overlap bowl by 1 inch. Cut off excess pastry shell. Cut slits on top of pastry shell to allow steam to escape. Place on baking sheet for easy handling. Bake for 1 hour or until crust is golden brown. Serve immediately.

Marinated Lemon Chicken Breasts

Yield: Serves 8

4 garlic cloves, minced
1 tablespoon canola oil
1 tablespoon sugar
1 tablespoon chopped fresh rosemary
2 teaspoons fresh thyme
2 teaspoons grated lemon rind
3/4 teaspoon coarsely ground black pepper, divided
1 teaspoon salt, divided
4 14 ounce bone-in chicken breasts, cut in half crosswise or thighs
1/2 cup fresh lemon juice
2 tablespoons olive oil
1 tablespoon red wine vinegar
2 teaspoons honey mustard

Combine, garlic, oil, sugar, rosemary, thyme, lemon rind, 1/4 teaspoon pepper and 1/2 teaspoon salt in large bowl; add chicken and toss until chicken is well coated; cover and refrigerate overnight or up to 24 hours. Preheat broiler or grill. Place chicken on large rimmed baking sheet or grill rack. Broil or grill 16 minutes, turning once. Meanwhile, combine lemon juice, olive oil, vinegar, honey mustard, 1/2 teaspoon salt and 1/2 teaspoon pepper in a medium bowl; whisk. Baste chicken with lemon juice mixture. Broil 8 more minutes, turning and basting twice, until an instant-read meat thermometer inserted into thickest part of breast registers 165 degrees.

Baked Chicken Breast

MARINADE
1 16 ounce bottle creamy French dressing
1 medium size can cranberry sauce
1 package onion dip

CHICKEN
6 skinless, boneless chicken breasts

Combine first 3 ingredients to make marinade. Dip chicken into marinade. Bake in ovenproof dish at 350 degrees for 20 to 25 minutes.

Baked Pomegranate Chicken Recipe

The traditional Persian dish, Khoresh Fesonjan, is cooked on top of the stove with ground walnuts. This recipe is for a baked Pomegranate chicken.

- 2 teaspoons cumin
- 1 1/2 teaspoons coriander
- 1 1/2 teaspoons cinnamon
- 1/2 teaspoon cayenne pepper
- 1/2 teaspoon black pepper
- 1 teaspoon salt, to taste
- 6 skinless, boneless chicken breasts and thighs
- 1 to 2 teaspoons garlic, minced
- 16 ounce bottle pomegranate juice
- 1/2 cup balsamic vinegar
- 2 tablespoons honey
- 2 tablespoons flour

Combine all dry herbs and spices; mix together. Put chicken in bowl with garlic. Coat chicken with spice mixture. Mix thoroughly so chicken is evenly coated. Pour in pomegranate juice, balsamic vinegar and add honey. Marinate overnight in fridge. The next day, drain all pomegranate marinade into a saucepan. Transfer chicken to a 13x9 baking dish. Bake, covered, at 350 degrees for 1 hour. While chicken is cooking, place marinade over medium-high heat and bring to boil. Add flour to help thicken sauce. Reduce pomegranate marinade by about two thirds, or until it forms a slightly thickened glaze. Spoon glaze over chicken 5 minutes before chicken is done; bake another 5 minutes. Transfer chicken to a serving platter.

Variation: Add fresh pomegranate on top. Also add apricots and prunes.

Curry Chicken Breast & Mushroom Rice with Saffron

Yield: Serves 10
Prep: Most of these items are found in Middle Eastern stores.

4 cups basmati or long-grain rice
4 teaspoons salt
2 1/4 teaspoons saffron (Spanish or Iranian), divided
7 tablespoons grape seed oil, divided
4 medium size onions, finely diced
1 pound boneless, skinless chicken breasts (cut in 1 inch cubes)
1 teaspoon garlic powder
2 tablespoons curry paste (medium or high heat)
2 teaspoons curry powder
1/2 pound mushrooms, sliced
1 medium size green bell pepper, julienned
1 medium size red bell pepper (sweet), julienned
1 medium size yellow bell pepper, julienned

Wash rice in strainer with warm water at least twice. Bring pot of water to boil. Pour in rice with 4 teaspoons of salt. Let it boil until rice is longer and tender (about 3 to 4 minutes). Strain rice and rinse with cold water. Add 1/4 cup water and 1/4 teaspoon saffron to pot. Pour rice into pot, over water and saffron. Cook on high heat until steam comes up. Add 4 tablespoons oil and lower heat. Cook for at least 45 minutes. Use 1 tablespoon oil to sauté onions and chicken breast on high heat, stirring constantly, until onions are translucent. Stir in 1 1/2 teaspoons saffron, garlic powder, curry paste and curry powder, one at a time. Cook 30 minutes on low to medium-heat, stirring periodically. Sauté mushrooms and peppers in a separate pan with remaining 2 tablespoons oil.

To make saffron rice: mix 1/2 teaspoon of saffron with 3 teaspoons hot water. Add half of cooked rice from above. On a large flat dish, spread a layer of white rice, a layer of chicken curry and a layer of peppers and mushrooms. Repeat layers and design top layer with saffron rice, mushrooms and peppers.

Chicken Hungarian

Yield: Serves 6

4 large onions, sliced
1/2 cup non-dairy margarine
2 garlic cloves, minced
3 tablespoons sweet paprika
6 boneless, skinless chicken-breast halves
1 cup rosé wine
salt and pepper, to taste
1 cup non-dairy sour cream

Place onions and margarine in large skillet; sauté onions until transparent. Add garlic and paprika; blend together; sauté 1 minute more. Add chicken breasts to mixture and sauté. Spoon onions over breasts. Add wine, salt and pepper; simmer until tender; about 30 minutes. Remove chicken to warm platter. Blend non-dairy sour cream into pan mixture, thicken with flour, if necessary. Return chicken to skillet. Serve with rice or noodles.

Hint: Good reheated.

Chicken Piccata

1/2 cup flour
1/4 to 1/2 teaspoon each: seasoned salt, pepper and garlic powder
8 to 10 boneless chicken breasts, flattened
2+ tablespoons olive oil
3 to 4 lemon slices, garnish
fresh parsley (chopped), garnish

Put flour and seasonings in a plastic bag and coat chicken breasts. Put olive oil in pan and sauté chicken breasts until lightly browned. Remove from pan.

Scrape bottom of pan and add:
4 to 5 tablespoons Madeira wine
3 tablespoons fresh lemon juice
1/2 4 ounce jar capers

Simmer for 5 minutes. Spray roasting pan with nonstick spray; place chicken breasts in pan. Pour sauce over chicken; lay 1/4 slice of lemon on each breast. Sprinkle with parsley. Bake at 350 degrees for 30 to 45 minutes.

Chicken with Apricots and Olives

12 boneless, skinless chicken breast halves (6 whole breasts, halved)
1 cup Kalamata or niçoise olives, drained
6 ounces dried apricots
1 cup dried figs, optional
1 cup dry vermouth
1/2 cup drained caper berries or capers
1 teaspoon grated orange peel
2 1/2 cups apricot jam, melted, divided
1/4 cup white wine vinegar
3 tablespoons dry basil leaves (not fresh)
2 tablespoons olive oil
6 cloves garlic, pressed or minced
orange slices for garnish
parsley, garnish

Preheat oven to 400 degrees. In a large bowl, combine chicken, olives, apricots, vermouth, capers, orange peel, 1 1/2 cups apricot jam, vinegar, basil, oil and garlic. Cover; chill overnight, stirring once. Arrange chicken in single layer in pan. Pour marinade over chicken. Evenly drizzle remaining 1 cup melted apricot jam over chicken. Bake, uncovered, for 30 to 35 minutes, basting once. Garnish with orange slices and parsley.

Variation: If made ahead, bring back to room temperature; reheat, loosely covered.

Chicken, Peppers and Pasta in a Skillet

Yield: Serves 2

1 cup rotini pasta, uncooked
8 ounces boneless, skinless chicken breasts, cut into bite-size pieces
1/2 medium green pepper, cut into thin strips
1/4 cup onion, chopped
1/2 teaspoon Italian seasoning
2 garlic cloves, diced
1 cup marinara sauce

Cook rotini as directed on package. Drain. Set aside. Spray large skillet with cooking spray. Add chicken. Cook and stir 5 minutes. Add green pepper, onion, Italian seasoning and garlic cloves. Cook until chicken is cooked through and vegetables are tender. Add marinara sauce and rotini. Mix well. Cook until heated through, stirring occasionally.

Apricot-Currant Chicken

Yield: Serves 8-12

8 to 12 boneless, skinless chicken breasts, (3 to 4 pounds)
 or a mixture of boneless, skinless chicken breasts and boneless, skinless chicken thighs
salt and freshly ground black pepper, to taste
powdered ginger
1 1/2 cups orange marmalade
1 1/2 cups apple juice
1/2 cup orange juice
8 ounces dried apricots
1/2 cup dried currants, more or less
1/4 cup brown sugar

Preheat oven to 350 degrees. Place chicken in shallow roasting pan (I usually use a large aluminum foil pan); sprinkle with salt, pepper and ginger. Turn over and repeat on second side. Spread marmalade over chicken; pour juices into pan. Add apricots and currants to pan around chicken; sprinkle with brown sugar. Bake, basting frequently, 35 to 40 minutes, until chicken is done. Place on warmed serving platter; pour some juices over top. Place remaining juices in a sauce boat and serve immediately.

Peach Glazed Chicken

cooking spray
1 teaspoon olive oil
1 pound small, boneless, skinless chicken breasts
1/2 cup peach preserves
2 tablespoons balsamic vinegar
1 green onion, chopped
1/4 teaspoon freshly ground pepper

Coat nonstick skillet with cooking spray; add oil and heat over medium-high heat. Add chicken; sauté 5 minutes on each side or until done (depending on thickness of chicken), remove from pan; set aside; keep warm. Reduce heat to low, add peach preserves, vinegar, green onion and pepper; stir constantly until onion is tender and preserves are melted. Return chicken to pan; coat with sauce. Serve with sauce spooned over chicken.

Variation: Can use bone-in chicken breasts. Sauté on both sides; bake for 45 minutes at 350 degrees.

Lemon-Pepper Balsamic Chicken

1 pound chicken cutlets or boneless, skinless chicken breasts
2 teaspoons lemon-pepper seasoning
1 1/2 teaspoons olive oil
1/3 cup balsamic vinegar
1/4 cup chicken broth
2 garlic cloves, minced
1 tablespoon pareve margarine

Place chicken breasts between two sheets waxed paper; with meat mallet, lightly pound to 1/4 inch thickness. Press lemon-pepper seasoning evenly on both sides of chicken. In large fry pan, heat olive oil to medium-temperature. Add chicken; cook 7 minutes on each side, turning once. Remove chicken; keep warm. Mix together vinegar, broth and garlic; add to fry pan. Cook over medium-high heat, stirring and scraping up brown bits, about 2 minutes or until mixture is reduced and syrupy. Add margarine. Stir to melt. Return chicken to pan; turn over in sauce to coat both sides. To serve, spoon remaining sauce over chicken. As with all chicken recipes, do not overcook.

Almond "Duck" Chicken

6 chicken breasts, boneless and skinless
10 to 12 ounces duck sauce
2 to 4 ounces slivered or sliced almonds

Place a single layer of chicken breasts in 9x13 ovenproof baking dish or any appropriate size aluminum foil pan. Spoon duck sauce over chicken; scatter almonds over chicken. Bake at 350 degrees for 35 to 40 minutes, depending on thickness of chicken breasts. Do not overcook.

For large crowds, I use two large aluminum foil roasting pans for 24 chicken breasts, a full jar of sauce and 8 to 10 ounces of almonds. It freezes well. Great for a large group on Shabbat or Passover.

The duck sauce is available in the kosher department at supermarkets or at a kosher butcher shop. Serve this with a rice dish.

Chicken in Olive Sauce

8 chicken breasts (or 2 small chickens cut up)
salt, pepper and paprika
1/3 cup flour, plus 2 tablespoons
3 tablespoons olive oil
1/2 cup dry sherry
2 onions, sliced
2 cloves garlic, minced
1/2 pound mushrooms, sliced
1 1/2 cups chicken broth
2 tablespoons tomato paste
1 cup pitted green olives, rinsed and sliced
1 bay leaf
2 ripe tomatoes, chopped

Season chicken with salt, pepper and paprika. Dredge in flour. Heat olive oil in a large skillet and brown chicken on all sides. Remove to large baking dish. Pour sherry over chicken. Using drippings from browning chicken, sauté onion and garlic until soft. Add mushrooms and cook until golden. Dissolve 2 tablespoons flour in chicken broth; blend until smooth. Add to sautéed vegetables and stir until smooth and slightly thickened. Add tomato paste, olives, pepper to taste and bay leaf. Heat to boil, stirring occasionally. Pour sauce over chicken, cover with foil; bake at 350 degrees for 45 minutes. Add tomatoes during last 20 minutes. Uncover and bake 5 to 10 minutes more.

Easy Chicken Bake

1 cut up chicken or 4 to 6 chicken breasts, boneless
1 egg
seasoned bread crumbs
canola or vegetable oil for browning

Dip chicken in egg, then crumbs; brown in oil on top of stove. Layer on rack in a roasting pan and bake for 40 minutes at 350 degrees.

Lemon-Rosemary Chicken

2 medium lemons
1 tablespoon rosemary, fresh chopped or dried
2 teaspoons olive oil
2 teaspoons salt
1/4 teaspoon pepper, coarsely ground
1 garlic clove, minced
1 teaspoon paprika
1 pound chicken breast halves

From 1 lemon, grate peel to equal 2 teaspoons. Thinly slice half of second lemon; reserve slices for garnish. Squeeze juice from remaining 3 lemon halves into small bowl. Stir in lemon peel, rosemary, olive oil, salt, pepper, garlic and paprika. Spray heavy skillet-grill or 12-inch skillet with nonstick cooking spray. Heat skillet over medium-high heat until very hot. Meanwhile, toss chicken-breast halves with lemon rosemary mixture.

Place chicken breast halves in hot skillet; cook for 5 minutes, brushing with remaining lemon juice mixture in bowl. Turn chicken over; cook 5 minutes longer, until juices run clear when thickest part of chicken breast is pierced with knife. Garnish with lemon slices.

Variation: Can be cooked on the barbecue.

Dijon Honey Chicken

COATING
1/3 cup mayonnaise
1/3 cup Dijon mustard
1/3 cup honey

CHICKEN
6 to 8 chicken breasts

CRUMB MIXTURE
3/4 to 1 cup bread crumbs
3/4 to 1 cup canned French-fried onions
1/2 cup fresh parsley
1 teaspoon paprika

Combine mayonnaise, Dijon mustard and honey. Dip chicken in coating. Combine bread crumbs, onions, parsley and paprika in food processor. Dip chicken in crumb mixture, so that chicken has been dipped first in coating and then in crumb mixture. Bake at 350 degrees for 20 to 25 minutes.

Shabbat in a Pot

1 onion, diced
1 carrot, diced
1 zucchini, diced
5 garlic cloves, minced
olive or vegetable oil to cover bottom of pot
1 cup brown rice
1 14.5 ounce can stewed tomatoes, include liquid
1/4 cup tomato paste
1 chicken cut into serving pieces, skin removed
1 3/4 cups water
1 tablespoon soy sauce
salt to taste

In a large frying pan, sauté onion, carrot, zucchini and garlic in oil until soft. Add rice. Add stewed tomatoes and tomato paste. Place chicken on top; pour water and soy sauce over. Bring to boil; cover, lowering heat. Simmer about 1 hour and 45 minutes, or until liquid is absorbed. Add salt.

Serve with soup and salad.

Cranberry Chicken

1 fryer cut into eighths
salt and pepper
1 7 ounce can jellied cranberry sauce
2 tablespoons soy sauce
1 1/2 tablespoons lemon juice
2 tablespoons pareve margarine

Salt and pepper chicken to taste. Combine all other ingredients and heat until melted. It's quicker if you mush up cranberry sauce in can first and cut up margarine, into pieces. This can be done in a glass bowl in microwave. Pour some sauce on bottom of pan. Place chicken skin-side down and pour rest of sauce over. Bake at 425 degrees for 30 minutes. Turn chicken skin-side up; bake for an additional 20 minutes. Baste halfway through this time.

Variation: When chicken is done, cover tightly; bake for an additional 2 hours at 300 degrees. This can be done after chicken has cooled. If you cook chicken a day ahead, bring back to room temperature before doing this, or just cook at 350 degrees for 2 to 2 1/2 hours.

Note: When multiplying this recipe, use less and less margarine, per chicken. Never use more than 8 tablespoons margarine no matter how many chickens you use. Nothing tragic will happen if you forget to baste. If you skin the chicken, you'll get a low-fat version with no diminution of taste. If you do this, you may have to use more margarine. De-fat sauce and serve alongside chicken.

Mediterranean Chicken

Yield: Serves 6-8
Prep Time: 40 minutes, Bake 1 1/2 hours

1/2 cup flour
1 1/4 teaspoons salt
1 1/4 teaspoons pepper
2 teaspoons dried oregano
2 3 pound chickens, cut into 8 pieces
3 1/2 tablespoons olive oil, divided
3 onions, thinly sliced
1 1/2 teaspoons minced garlic
1 cup thinly sliced celery
1 cup thinly sliced carrots
1/2 cup dry white wine
1 14.5 ounce can no-salt diced tomatoes
1 14.5 ounce can low-salt chicken broth
2 tablespoons tomato paste
12 Kalamata olives
1/2 cup minced parsley mixed with 1 teaspoon dried oregano

Heat oven to 375 degrees. Set aside a 4 quart casserole or baking dish. Combine flour, salt, pepper and oregano in a large plastic bag. Coat raw chicken pieces a few at a time, shaking off excess. Heat 1 1/2 tablespoons oil in nonstick skillet over medium to high-heat. Brown first chicken on all sides for 6 minutes. Add 1 1/2 tablespoons oil to skillet for second chicken. Transfer to casserole. Add any remaining flour mixture to casserole. Add remaining 1/2 tablespoon oil to skillet. When hot, add onions, garlic, celery and carrots. Cook, stirring often, until onions are soft, about 6 minutes. Add wine, tomatoes, broth, tomato paste, olives and parsley mixture. Stir well. Bring to a boil, then pour over chicken. Bake covered for 1 hour. Bake uncovered for an additional 30 minutes. Cool, refrigerate up to 3 days, covered airtight. To serve, reheat covered at 350 degrees for 45 minutes. Serve over hot macaroni with extra sauce on top. Can be frozen.

MACARONI WITH FRESH DILL & GREEN ONION

Prep Time: 5 minutes to prep; 15 minutes total cooking time.

3/4 pounds elbow macaroni
salt (for boiling water)
3 tablespoons pareve margarine
1/3 cup snipped fresh dill
2 small green onions, sliced
salt
ground pepper

Cook macaroni in boiling salted water, according to package directions. Meanwhile, melt margarine, stir in dill and green onions. Drain macaroni, stir in margarine mixture and generously season with salt and pepper.

Note: Needs to be done at least 1 day ahead, reheated in microwave.

Four-Way Chicken

1 chicken, cut up
4 tablespoons margarine
4 tablespoons honey
4 tablespoons soy sauce
4 tablespoons lemon juice

Place chicken in baking dish, skin side down. Combine ingredients in saucepan; cook over low heat until dissolved. Pour over chicken. Bake uncovered at 350 degrees for 1 hour, turning once and basting frequently until covered with a rich brown sauce.

Note: The kabbalists (Jewish mystics) who flocked to the Upper Galilee mountain town of Safed after the Spanish Inquisition read great significance into combinations of numbers and letters. Their synagogues are still to be found in modern Safed, which is also known for its beautiful scenery, artists colony and resort hotels. The combinations of 4 in this recipe contain no mystery-just good eating!

Hodge Podge Chicken

16 pieces of chicken
1 teaspoon salt
1/2 teaspoon pepper
1 tablespoon paprika
1 18 ounce can pineapple chunks
1 8 ounce can tomato sauce
1 6 ounce can frozen orange juice concentrate, thawed
6 cloves garlic, minced
1/4 cup packed brown sugar
1 teaspoon cinnamon
1/2 teaspoon dry mustard

Sprinkle chicken on all sides with salt, pepper and paprika. Place in large 12x18 roasting pan. Drain pineapple and reserve juice. Mix 1 cup pineapple juice with tomato sauce, orange juice, garlic, sugar, cinnamon and mustard; pour over chicken. Bake at 375 degrees for about 1 1/2 hours, basting every 15 minutes. Add pineapple chunks last 5 minutes. Serve over bed of rice.

Oven Fried Chicken with Lemon Sauce

SAUCE

1 tablespoon soy sauce
1/2 teaspoon salt
1/2 teaspoon pepper
1/4 cup vegetable oil
1/2 cup lemon juice
2 teaspoons grated lemon peel
2 to 3 cloves of garlic, crushed
1 teaspoon sugar

Combine all ingredients; refrigerate at least 1 hour before using.

CHICKEN

1/2 cup flour
1 teaspoon salt
1/2 teaspoon pepper
2 teaspoons paprika
3 pounds chicken pieces
1/4 cup vegetable oil

Combine flour, salt, pepper and paprika. Coat chicken pieces well with mixture. Place chicken in single layer in ovenproof dish. Sprinkle with oil; bake uncovered at 350 degrees for 30 minutes. Turn chicken; pour sauce over chicken. Bake a further 30 minutes or until golden brown.

Variation 1: Use orange peel instead of lemon and juice of one orange.

Variation 2: Add 1 pound green beans as side dish. Boil green beans for 4 to 5 minutes. Drain hot water; rinse with cold water. Heat 2 tablespoons olive oil in a large skillet. Add 1 large shallot, finely chopped, sauté until golden. Add green beans to shallot and oil mixture; stir for 1 minute. Serve with chicken. Very delicious!

Stuffed Bell Peppers

Yield: Serves 4

1 1/2 cups white rice
1 pound ground turkey
1 tablespoon cumin
1 tablespoon chili powder
1 tablespoon minced garlic
1/2 cup diced yellow onions
1/2 cup diced red bell pepper
1/2 cup diced green bell pepper
1 whole chipotle chili, minced
1 can diced tomatoes
1 cup black beans, drained and rinsed
1 teaspoon salt
1/2 teaspoon pepper
4 whole green bell peppers
1 cup canned vegetable broth

Cook white rice and reserve. In a large sauté pan, cook ground turkey with cumin, chili powder, garlic, onions, green and red bell peppers. Combine chipotle peppers with tomatoes and add onion/pepper mixture. Add black beans and white rice; stir well. Taste; season with salt and pepper, if needed. Remove from heat; let sit for 10 minutes to allow ground turkey mixture to cool. While turkey mixture is cooling, prepare 4 whole peppers for stuffing. Rinse peppers and cut top off each pepper. Scoop out seeds and membrane, being careful not to break pepper. Fill each pepper with ground turkey mixture and place in baking dish. Once baking dish is filled with all 4 stuffed green peppers, add canned vegetable broth to pan; cover with plastic wrap and then with aluminum foil (the plastic wrap will not allow the tin foil to stick to the peppers). Bake stuffed peppers for 30 minutes at 350 degrees.

Chicken Kids Like

Yield: Serves 4-6

2 1/2 to 3 pounds chicken, cut in 8 pieces
1 cup thinly sliced onion
2 cloves garlic, minced
2 cups sliced mushrooms
2 medium tomatoes, chopped
1/3 cup dry white wine
2 tablespoons balsamic vinegar
1 teaspoon crumbled dry thyme
1/2 teaspoon salt
1/2 teaspoon freshly ground pepper

Spray large nonstick skillet with nonstick cooking spray; add chicken pieces and cook over medium-heat until browned on both sides, about 6 to 8 minutes. Transfer to 9x13 inch baking pan. Preheat oven to 350 degrees. Place onion and garlic in same skillet; sauté until soft. Add mushrooms; cook 1 minute longer. Stir in remaining ingredients and cook 1 minute more. Pour vegetable mixture evenly over chicken. Cover with aluminum foil; bake 25 minutes. Remove foil; bake 15 minutes longer, or until chicken is cooked.

Zucchini-Turkey Burgers

1 pound skinless turkey, ground
1 medium zucchini, shredded
1/4 cup minced red onion
1/4 teaspoon salt
1/2 teaspoon freshly ground pepper

Spray a nonstick ridged grill pan or fry pan with cooking spray. Heat over medium heat. Combine all ingredients, shape into 4 patties and grill until brown on outside and no longer pink in center, about 7 minutes on each side.

Variation: Serve with Dijon mustard and grilled onions.

Barbecued Boneless Turkey Breast

Very easy, fast and delicious

1 boneless turkey breast
6 ounces small carrots (the kind you give to your kids as a snack)
1 onion in chunks
1 box cremini mushrooms
4 tablespoons (or more) poppy-seed salad dressing, divided
2 to 5 cloves fresh garlic, minced, divided
(quantity depends on size of cloves and size of turkey breast)
seasoned salt, to taste
paprika

Spread out a piece of heavy duty aluminum foil (large enough to wrap up turkey breast with vegetables added). Place turkey breast skin side down. Mix carrots, onion and mushrooms. Pour 1 to 2 tablespoons of salad dressing over turkey breast and put half of garlic on top. Sprinkle seasoned salt rather generously all over. Sprinkle lesser amount of paprika all over. Turn turkey breast over and repeat salad dressing and seasonings. Lift turkey breast; put most of vegetables underneath and put rest around turkey breast. Close foil tightly. Put package in foil pan. Place in barbecue on medium and cook for 30 minutes. Turn package over; cook 30 minutes. Let turkey rest closed for 15 minutes or so. Open package carefully to keep juice from pouring out. Slice turkey, put on platter with vegetables and pour some of juice over it.

Variation 1: Can be cooked in oven at 400 degrees.

Variation 2: Add orange juice and Dijon mustard for an interesting tangy flavor.

Stuffed Cornish Hens

6 Cornish hens (have the butcher split them lengthwise in half while still frozen, adapt numbers as needed). One Cornish hen can easily serve 2 people.
salt
pepper
paprika
1 box stuffing (prepare according to directions)
frozen orange juice, thawed
apricot preserves or duck sauce

Clean and wash defrosted hens, gently removing all extra goodies found in cavity. Remove fat and extra skin (skin that is hanging). Leave skin on breast and thigh. Sprinkle top of Cornish hens lightly with salt, pepper and paprika; place in refrigerator while you prepare stuffing. Pack open cavity of each Cornish hen half with stuffing. Place stuffed Cornish hens in baking pan, close together but do not overlap them. Bake at 350 degrees for 1 hour. Final touch; mix orange juice and equal amount of apricot preserves or duck sauce. Pour mixture over stuffed hens and bake 20 to 30 minutes more.

Marinated Chicken

Pesach or every day

1 bottle non-fat garlic salad dressing
1 bottle balsamic vinaigrette salad dressing
1 bottle Passover white wine
several squeezed lemons
2 to 3 packages chicken parts
1 jar apricot jam
3 sprigs fresh thyme, minced

Mix both salad dressings, wine and lemon juice. Pour over chicken parts and marinate for a few hours. Remove chicken from marinade and save marinade. Broil chicken parts until lightly browned. Heat saved marinade with apricot jam and thyme. Bake chicken at 350 degrees for 30 minutes. Serve with marinade over chicken.

Vegetables and Rice

Vegetables and Rice

Carrot Soufflé

1 pound carrots, cut in chunks
3 eggs
3 tablespoons flour (or matzah cake meal)
1 teaspoon vanilla
1 stick margarine
1 dash nutmeg

Cook carrots until tender. Blend cooked carrots and eggs in a food processor. Add remaining ingredients. Put in a deep ovenproof dish or soufflé bowl. Bake for 40 minutes at 350 degrees.

TOPPING

1/2 cup chopped pecans
3 tablespoons brown sugar

Mix pecans and sugar. Add topping to carrot mixture and bake 5 to 10 more minutes.

Variation: Double ingredients, bake in a 9×13 dish.

Green Beans and Peanuts

3 tablespoons olive oil
1 large onion, chopped
3/4 cup peanuts, unsalted and skinned
3 to 4 cloves garlic, chopped
1 1/2 pounds green beans
salt and pepper, to taste

Heat oil in a skillet and sauté onions. After 5 minutes, add nuts and garlic; continue to sauté until onions are translucent. Add green beans, salt and black pepper. Continue to sauté until beans are tender. Serve hot.

Almonds and Broccoli Stir-Fry

1 pound broccoli
1 teaspoon sesame seeds
3 tablespoons olive oil
1 teaspoon coriander
2 tablespoons almonds, slivered
1 clove garlic, crushed
1/2 teaspoon ginger, ground
2 tablespoons red wine vinegar
1 tablespoon soy sauce
2 teaspoons sesame oil

Cut broccoli into small florets. Microwave 4 to 5 minutes. Toast sesame seeds and remove from pan. Heat oil in pan; add coriander and almonds. Stir quickly over medium heat about 1 minute, until almonds are golden. Add garlic, ginger and broccoli to pan. Stir-fry over high heat until tender. Remove from heat. Stir in vinegar, soy sauce and sesame oil. Serve immediately, sprinkled with toasted sesame seeds.

Corn Kugel

3 14.7 ounce cans creamed corn
1 15.2 ounce can whole kernel corn, drained
1/3 cup sugar
3/4 cup butter or pareve margarine
5 large eggs, lightly beaten
3/4 cup all-purpose flour
1 1/2 teaspoons baking powder
1 1/4 cups milk or soy milk (regular or vanilla)
2 teaspoons vanilla

Preheat oven to 350 degrees. Lightly grease a 9x13 inch baking dish; set aside. In a large bowl, combine all ingredients and mix well. Make sure flour and baking powder are well incorporated; there should be no lumps. Pour into prepared dish. Bake uncovered 1 1/2 hours or until top is golden brown and center is set.

Aunt Leah's Cranberry Relish

Yield: Serves 10

3 large apples
3 navel oranges
1 1/2 cups water
1 1/4 cups sugar
1 12 ounce package cranberries
fresh ginger, grated

Peel and core apples, slice thin. Grate orange peel and set aside. Continue peeling oranges and divide into sections. Bring water and sugar to a boil. Add fruit and simmer for 15 minutes. Add cranberries and cook for 25 to 30 minutes, until cranberries burst. Pour into bowl. Refrigerate. Add freshly grated ginger and freshly grated orange peel.

Connie's Baked Eggplant

Yield: Serves 8-10

1 eggplant, sliced in 1/2 inch slices
salt to taste
olive oil
1 8 ounce can tomato sauce
5 to 6 cloves garlic, sliced
celery leaves

Salt eggplant; let stand about 30 minutes, then rinse. Sauté both sides in olive oil until golden, then place in baking dish in single layer. Spread tomato sauce on each slice and top with garlic slices, then celery leaves. Bake at 350 degrees about 30 minutes. Can be served warm or cold.

Peas with Mushrooms

1/2 pound fresh mushrooms, sliced
2 tablespoons onions, sliced
1 tablespoon butter
1/4 teaspoon dried marjoram
1/4 teaspoon salt
1/8 teaspoon pepper
dash nutmeg
1 10 ounce package frozen peas, cooked

In pot, over medium heat, sauté mushrooms and onions in butter. Add marjoram, salt, pepper and nutmeg. Mix well. Add peas and heat through.

Mushrooms and Spinach

Yield: Serves 2

2 tablespoons butter
1/2 cup chopped onions
5 ounces mushrooms
1 6 ounce bag of spinach
salt and pepper, to taste

In a large skillet, heat butter until hot. Add onions; sauté over high heat, stirring until soft. Add mushrooms; sauté over high heat, until brown. Stir in spinach, cover pan; cook 1 to 2 minutes or until spinach is cooked down and tender. Salt and pepper to taste. Cook uncovered for 1 minute more.

Ratatouille

Yield: Serves 8

1 onion, sliced
1 green pepper, sliced
1 red pepper, sliced
1/4 cup oil
2 tomatoes, peeled and sliced
2 zucchini, sliced
1 large eggplant, peeled and cubed
3 cloves garlic, minced
1/8 teaspoon oregano
salt and pepper, to taste

Brown onion and peppers in oil. Add tomatoes, zucchini and eggplant. Cover. Cook (about 30 minutes) over medium-heat or until vegetables are tender. Add garlic, oregano, salt and pepper. Simmer for 10 minutes more. Serve hot or at room temperature.

Succotash

3 tablespoons olive oil
2 shallots, chopped
2 10 ounce packages frozen corn
2 10 ounce packages frozen lima beans
3/4 cup low salt chicken broth
2 teaspoons chopped marjoram
1 pint cherry tomatoes, halved
salt and pepper, to taste

Heat oil in skillet on medium heat. Add shallots. Cook for 3 minutes. Stir in corn, lima beans, broth and marjoram. Cook, uncovered, for 14 minutes. Add tomatoes. Season with salt and pepper. Serve immediately.

Yellow Squash Soufflé

2 10 ounce packages frozen yellow squash
1/2 cup milk
4 eggs
1 cup butter, melted
1/2 cup sugar
1 cup flour
1 teaspoon baking powder
1 teaspoon vanilla
1 teaspoon salt
cinnamon

Defrost squash. Using a mixer on medium speed, combine all ingredients, except cinnamon. Spray a medium-sized soufflé dish. Pour mixture into dish; sprinkle with cinnamon. Bake at 350 degrees for 1 hour.

Roasted Brussels Sprouts

Yield: Serves 6-8

1 1/2 pounds Brussels sprouts, ends trimmed, yellow leaves removed
3 tablespoons olive oil
1 teaspoon salt
1/2 teaspoon freshly ground black pepper

Preheat oven to 400 degrees. Place Brussels sprouts, olive oil, salt and pepper in a large bowl. Mix well until all sprouts are covered evenly. Pour onto baking sheet and place on center oven rack. Roast 30 to 45 minutes, shaking pan every 5 to 7 minutes for even browning. Reduce heat when necessary to prevent burning. Brussels sprouts should be darkest brown, almost black, when done. Adjust seasoning with salt, if necessary. Serve immediately.

Roasted Broccoli

1 head of broccoli
1 to 2 teaspoons salt
1/4 cup olive oil
large plastic bag

Preheat oven to 400 degrees. Separate broccoli into small "florets." Combine salt and olive oil in a plastic bag; put in broccoli; shake well. Spread single layer on baking sheet; roast about 30 minutes or so, until brown and crisp.

Variation: Can also do this with cauliflower or Brussels sprouts.

Roasted Cauliflower

Yield: Serves 6 as a side dish

1 large head of cauliflower, cut into bite-size pieces (about 4 cups)
1 red pepper, cut into 1 inch pieces
3 tablespoons extra virgin olive oil
salt and pepper, to taste
1 onion, cut into 1 inch pieces, optional
fresh rosemary, optional

Preheat oven to 375 degrees. Line a baking sheet with foil and spray lightly with cooking spray. Spread cauliflower and red pepper on baking sheet; drizzle with the olive oil. Season with salt and pepper. Roast in oven for approximately 40 minutes or until soft and lightly browned on edges.

Variation: Add coarsely chopped onion. Roast onion for 30 minutes before adding vegetables, so all will be done at same time. Serve warm or at room temperature. Fresh rosemary might add another layer of flavor.

Oven Roasted Root Vegetables

Yield: Serves 10

1 1/2 pounds small red or white thin-skinned potatoes, cut into quarters
2 cups baby carrots
1 8 ounce bag frozen pearl onions (you can use fresh) or substitute 2 onions, quartered
1 teaspoon dried thyme
1 teaspoon dried rosemary or 2 teaspoons fresh rosemary
1/4 cup olive oil
3 tablespoons balsamic vinegar
salt and pepper, to taste

Preheat oven to 425 degrees. Line a 12x15 baking pan or large baking sheet with foil. In a large mixing bowl, combine potatoes, carrots, onions, dried herbs and olive oil. Roast vegetables 1 hour, stirring at least twice, until tender when pierced with a fork. Drizzle with balsamic vinegar; heat through another 5 minutes. Add salt and pepper, to taste.

Variation: Add parsnips, whole beets and whole cloves of garlic.

Oven Roasted Plum Tomatoes

Yield: Serves 24
Prep Time: 10 minutes
Cooking Time: 50 minutes

nonstick spray
12 large plum tomatoes (about 2 1/2 pounds), halved lengthwise
salt and pepper
1/4 cup extra virgin olive oil

FILLINGS
mozzarella, marinated in herb olive oil with pesto sauce drizzled over or
artichoke antipasto or
goat cheese with chives

Preheat oven to 400 degrees. Spray large baking sheet with nonstick spray. Remove seeds and juice from tomato halves. Arrange cut side up on baking sheet; sprinkle lightly with salt and pepper, then drizzle with oil. Roast until slightly charred and tender, about 50 minutes. Cool completely on sheet. Spoon filling into each tomato half.

Zucchini Casserole

Yield: Serves 4. Can be doubled or tripled. If tripled, serves 14.

1 1/2 pounds zucchini
1 cup chopped onion
4 tablespoons butter or margarine
2 eggs
1/2 tablespoon salt
1/3 teaspoon pepper

Peel, wash and dice zucchini. Add onion; bring to boil in 3/4 cup water. Simmer until barely tender; drain very well. Add butter/margarine, well-beaten eggs, salt and pepper. Mix thoroughly. Place in a casserole. Bake at 325 degrees for 30 minutes.

Zucchini and Tomatoes

My mom always made this as a side dish whenever zucchini was in season. I grow zucchini in my vegetable garden and I love to make this dish with freshly picked zucchini.

2 tablespoons vegetable oil
1 medium onion, diced
2 cloves garlic, minced
1 stalk celery, cut in 1/2 inch pieces
1 pound zucchini, sliced in 1/2 inch circles
1 14.5 ounce can stewed tomatoes
1 teaspoon sugar
2 teaspoons granulated garlic
1 teaspoon salt
1 teaspoon black pepper
1 11 ounce can whole kernel sweet corn

Heat oil in skillet, sauté onions until wilted, then add garlic and celery, sauté until wilted. Add zucchini. When vegetables are tender, add tomatoes and seasonings. Add corn; simmer 10 minutes, until heated through. This will serve 6 people.

Variation: May be served hot or cold.

Almodrote (Baked Zucchini)

4 medium zucchini (2 pounds)
6 large eggs
1 8 ounce carton cottage cheese
1/4 cup flour
1 teaspoon baking powder
1 cup Parmesan cheese, divided
1/4 cup feta cheese, crumbled, optional
salt and pepper
1 tablespoon vegetable oil
1/4 cup matzah meal

Preheat oven to 400 degrees. Grate zucchini and squeeze out liquid really well. Beat eggs. To eggs, add zucchini, cottage cheese, flour, baking powder, 3/4 cup Parmesan cheese, feta (optional), salt and pepper, to taste. Combine thoroughly. Pour oil into 9x13 pan or casserole and heat in oven until hot. Remove pan carefully, sprinkle bottom of pan with matzah meal. Carefully pour zucchini mixture into pan. Sprinkle remaining Parmesan cheese over top of mixture. Bake for 1 hour. It will be golden brown on top.

Almodrote is a famous Sephardic recipe. It is great served hot or cold. It is often served with sour cream.

Eve's Mashed Potatoes

4 to 6 baking potatoes
1 8 ounce package cream cheese
1 cup sour cream
butter
salt and pepper, to taste
paprika

Cook potatoes with skin on or off in boiling water until soft; drain well. Return to bowl; mash potatoes. Add cream cheese and sour cream. Put in soufflé dish and refrigerate. Remove at least 1 hour before baking at 350 degrees for 20 to 30 minutes. Sprinkle top with butter, salt and pepper, to taste, and paprika.

Variation: Can use margarine instead of butter, non-fat sour cream and Neufchâtel cheese instead of cream cheese.

Roasted Potatoes

1/2 cup Dijon honey mustard
1/2 cup olive oil
3 pounds baking potatoes, cut into 1 1/2 inch cubes
2 medium onions, sliced
chopped fresh parsley for garnish
salt, to taste

In small bowl, combine mustard and oil. In large bowl, combine potatoes, onions and mustard mixture, toss well to coat. Spread in baking pan. Bake at 400 degrees for 1 hour or until potatoes are tender and crispy, stirring once. Transfer to serving platter. Garnish with parsley and salt, to taste.

Mashed Sweet Potatoes with Dried Apples

2 1/2 pounds sweet potatoes, scrubbed
2/3 cup dried apples, chopped
1/2 cup apple cider
4 tablespoons unsalted butter, softened
1 tablespoon lemon juice
coarse salt, to taste

Preheat oven to 450 degrees. Prick the potato skins in several places. Place whole potatoes on a sheet of heavy-duty aluminum foil or baking sheet. Bake until tender. Cooking times will vary according to size of potatoes. Most take 20 to 30 minutes. A good way to test for doneness is to probe potatoes with a skewer. Meanwhile, put apples and cider in a small saucepan. Simmer over low heat until most of liquid has been absorbed, so pan is almost dry, 10 to 15 minutes. Remove from heat. Peel sweet potatoes, holding them in a towel to protect your hands from heat. Drop them into a pot or large bowl. Smash flesh with a heavy wire whisk, then whisk until smooth. Whisk in butter. Stir in apples and lemon juice. Season with salt, to taste. Serve warm.

Sweet Potato Soufflé in Orange Shell

3 medium yams (sweet potatoes)
1 cup brown sugar
1 cup crushed pineapple
2 eggs, well beaten
4 teaspoons melted butter
1/2 teaspoon cinnamon
1/2 teaspoon nutmeg
5 navel oranges
10 marshmallows

Peel sweet potatoes and cut into chunks, boil until fork-tender. Make filling: mash boiled potatoes and add ingredients, except for oranges and marshmallows. Cut oranges in half and scoop out orange, dry inside of orange. Beat potato mixture until creamy. Scoop into orange shells. Put shells in muffin tins. Bake in preheated 350 degree oven for 20 minutes or until light brown. Put 1 marshmallow on each soufflé. Return to oven and bake until marshmallow is puffed and lightly brown.

Sharon's Stuffins

1 cup liquid egg substitute, or two large eggs
1 cup low-sodium vegetable broth or kosher chicken broth
4 tablespoons light margarine
1/2 cup finely minced green or brown onions
1/2 cup chopped celery
1/2 cup shredded or finely chopped zucchini
1/2 cup chopped mushrooms
1/4 cup chopped fresh Italian flat-leaf parsley
1/2 cup finely chopped spinach
2 garlic cloves, finely minced
1 teaspoon poultry seasoning
1/4 teaspoon paprika
salt and pepper, to taste
1 loaf day-old bread cut into 1/2 inch cubes (challah works great!)

Preheat oven to 375 degrees. Coat 16 to 24 muffin cups with pareve cooking spray. Do not use paper liners. In a large bowl, combine egg substitute and broth. Melt margarine in a large frying pan. Sauté vegetables, beginning with onions and celery. When they soften, add zucchini, mushrooms, parsley, spinach and garlic. Add seasonings; continue to sauté until vegetables are just lightly golden in color. Add vegetables to egg and broth mixture; toss lightly. Next, add bread cubes; toss lightly. If stuffin mixture is too dry, simply add more broth. Mixture should be soft, but not mushy. Carefully spoon into muffin cups. Bake 20 to 25 minutes until golden in color and set. If there are any leftovers, these can be frozen and reheated for later use.

Currant Rice (Persian)

Tina, a member of the VBS Sisterhood Executive Board, has been making this traditional rice dish forever, as taught by her mother. This is the first time it's been written down.

- 1 to 2 tablespoons barberries
- 1 12 ounce package currant raisins
- 1 large onion, diced small
- 2 to 3 tablespoons cooking oil (canola or grape seed, not olive oil), divided
- 2 cups basmati rice
- 9 to 10 tablespoons salt, divided
- 1 1/3 tablespoons turmeric, divided
- 1/3 cup water
- 2 russet potatoes
- 1 to 2 tablespoons cumin

Barberries need to be cleaned carefully by hand (there are small stones in the dried berries), strained and rinsed, then washed again in a fine colander. Add currants and rinse again. Lightly brown onion in small amount of vegetable oil, add rinsed currants and barberries. Wash rice, add 4 to 5 tablespoons salt, then soak in cold water at least 30 minutes (may soak overnight in refrigerator or on counter); should be cool. Boil large pot of water, add 5 tablespoons salt. Drain excess water from rice; add to boiling water; add 1 tablespoon turmeric for color; stir occasionally. Boil for 7 minutes only. Do not boil any longer than this. Should be al dente. Use a stainless steel pot, not nonstick, for boiling rice. In medium-sized, nonstick pot, add 1/3 cup water and remainder of turmeric. Peel and cut potatoes into 1/4 inch thick slices; keep in bowl of water until ready to use. Drain; lay flat on bottom of nonstick pot. Drain rice; rinse in cold water. Spoon a layer of rice over potatoes. Sprinkle rice with a layer of barberry/currant mix. Sprinkle a layer of cumin. Add another layer of rice, then barberry/currant mix, then cumin. Finish with a final layer. Should look like a mini mountain. Use a wooden spoon handle to poke holes down into mountain. Place pot on stove top; cover; cook on high for about 10 minutes. Bottom layer will get crunchy. When mixture starts to generate steam, remove pot cover and add about 1 tablespoon additional oil. Cover, this time with a paper towel first to soak up steam, then put pot cover back on. Cook another 10 to 15 minutes. When finished, spoon out and layer onto a dish.

Rice with Golden Raisins

Yield: Serves 8

3 cups chicken broth
4 tablespoons olive oil
1/2 teaspoon turmeric
1/2 teaspoon curry
1 1/2 tablespoons soy sauce
1 1/2 cups uncooked white rice
1/2 cup seedless golden raisins
toasted almonds, garnish

Heat chicken broth, oil and seasonings. Let boil. Add rice and raisins, cover; cook 20 minutes. Garnish with toasted almonds.

Herbed Rice

Yield: Serves 6-8

1 bunch flat leaf parsley, washed and dried, stems removed
1 bunch cilantro, washed and dried, stems removed
3 tablespoons olive oil
1 onion, diced
1 1/2 cups basmati rice
1/2 cup fresh dill, snipped
1/4 cup fresh mint, minced
2 cups water
1/8 teaspoon saffron strands or 1/4 teaspoon turmeric
salt and pepper, to taste

Finely chop parsley and cilantro, set aside. Heat olive oil in a very large frying pan with a lid. Over medium heat, fry onions until soft and golden. While onions are cooking, rinse rice in water, drain. Repeat 2 more times, until water is clear.

In frying pan, add parsley, cilantro, dill and mint to onions along with water. Add saffron or turmeric; bring to a boil. Pour rice into herb mixture; stir to combine. Bring back to a boil, cover; reduce heat to a simmer. Cook rice for 20 minutes. Fluff with a fork, adding salt and pepper, to taste.

Mujadara Lentils and Rice (Pareve)

Yield: Serves 6-8

1 cup brown lentils
3 cups water
1 1/2 cups rice (Jasmine or Basmati)
1 teaspoon ground cumin
1 teaspoon ground coriander
1/4 teaspoon turmeric
6 to 7 cardamom pods
salt and pepper, to taste
1 tablespoon fresh ginger, minced

If you do not have these seasonings and spices, just use salt and pepper. The mujadara will still be a tasty and healthy meal.

Rinse lentils; drain. Put in large pot with water. Bring to a boil, then lower heat and simmer. Add rice and seasonings, cook another 15 minutes. Check after 10 minutes and add more water. It should not be too dry.

Variation: Serve with caramelized onions. We eat this with a chopped salad of tomatoes, cucumber and parsley with olive oil and lemon juice dressing.

CARAMELIZED ONION TOPPING

5 or 6 large onions for a lot of topping, or
2 or 3 large onions for less topping.
olive oil
salt and pepper, to taste

Cut onions in half; slice. There are 2 ways to prepare onions. Cook the onions in a frying pan on top of the stove, use olive oil and a little salt; sauté slowly until they are very brown. This takes a while. If you are making lots of onions, bake them. Preheat oven to 400 degrees. Line largest baking sheet you have with foil and drizzle with olive oil. Lay sliced onions on sheet; add more olive oil and a little salt and pepper. Roast in oven until brown, about 45 minutes to 1 hour, tossing from time to time.

Sephardic Onion Rice

This dish is common to Jews who came from Iraq, like my husband Mark's family. Mark's cousin calls it "Mama Rice."

Yield: Serves 6-8, can be doubled or cut in half

2 large onions
2 tablespoons corn oil for the rice, plus extra to brown the onions
2 cups long grain rice (Basmati rice is best)
3 cups water
salt, to taste

Chop onions into small pieces. Slowly brown onions in corn oil over low heat, stirring occasionally. This takes a long time, so get onions started; let them cook while you make rice. Onions should be very brown, almost burnt. Rinse rice in cold water a couple of times, to remove extra starch, then drain. Put rice into a nonstick pot with measured water, measured corn oil and salt. Cook rice uncovered over high heat until boiling, stirring occasionally. Keep boiling until water reduces slightly below rice level, then lower heat, cover pot and let simmer for 20 minutes. When rice is done, fluff with a fork and gently mix in browned onions together with oil they were cooked in.

Cracked Wheat Pilaf

Yield: Serves 6-8

2 cups cracked wheat or bulgur
1 medium onion, chopped
5 cups beef broth
1/4 cup pareve margarine, melted
1/4 cup minced parsley or 2 tablespoons dried parsley flakes
salt, to taste

Combine ingredients in crockpot; stir well. Cover; cook on low for 10 to 12 hours or on high for 3 to 4 hours, stirring occasionally.

Ta Chin, Persian Rice (Dairy)

2 cups basmati (long grain) rice
4 to 5 tablespoons salt
1 1/2 ounces barberries, cleaned and washed
cooking oil for sautéing
1 to 3 teaspoons sugar
1 1/2 pounds mushrooms
salt and pepper, to taste
1 tablespoon cooking oil
3 egg yolks
3 tablespoons plain yogurt
dash of saffron, ground

Wash rice, add salt, then soak in cold water at least 30 minutes (may soak overnight in fridge) or in a cool place. Boil a large stainless steel pot of water; add more salt, to taste. Drain excess water from rice; add to boiling water; stir occasionally. Boil for 7 to 10 minutes only. Do not boil any longer than this. Should be al dente. Drain rice in a fine colander; run cold water over it. Preheat oven to 400 degrees. Sauté barberries with a bit of oil, add sugar. Wash, slice, sauté mushrooms separately, add salt and pepper, to taste. In a bowl, mix 1/3 of drained rice with oil, egg yolks, yogurt, salt, pepper and saffron. Spread mixture on bottom of a glass ovenproof dish, then spread a layer of mushrooms and barberries. Spread another layer of plain rice, add a dash of saffron, another layer of mushrooms and barberries and so on. Save some of the barberries.

Cover glass dish with aluminum foil; cook in oven for 1 hour, then lower temperature to 350 degrees and cook for another 1 1/2 hours. Once ready (check bottom of glass dish for color and crispness of rice) remove from oven. Let it cool for a few minutes. Put a spare serving tray on top of glass dish and flip it over. Rice should freely and easily flip. You have colorful, crispy rice. Decorate with saved barberries.

Wild Rice

1 3 ounce package wild rice
1/8 pound pareve margarine
3/4 cup chopped onion
1/3 cup chopped celery
3/4 cup chopped pecans, optional
3/4 cup long-grain white rice
2 cups chicken broth
2 tablespoons soy sauce
1/8 teaspoon salt

Add wild rice to 1 cup water. Boil for 20 minutes and rinse. Sauté margarine, onion and celery in a large skillet. Add nuts and white rice. Fry mixture for a little longer. Stir in wild rice. Separately, bring chicken broth to a boil. Add soy sauce and salt to broth; mix. Then stir in rice. Put this over a low heat for 10 to 15 minutes to use as stuffing or bake at 350 degrees for 1 to 1 1/4 hours.

Wild Rice with Nuts and Raisins

Yield: Serves 6

This recipe tastes best served at room temperature. It is best made a day ahead to give the flavors a chance to develop. However, it can be made just a few hours before serving.

1 cup raw wild rice
5 1/2 cups chicken stock or water
1 cup pecan pieces
1 cup yellow raisins
grated rind of 1 orange
1/2 cup chopped fresh mint (extra mint leaves for garnish)
3 scallions, thinly sliced
1/4 cup extra virgin olive oil
1/3 cup orange juice
1 1/2 teaspoons salt
black pepper, to taste

Place rice in a strainer and rinse thoroughly. Place rice in a saucepan. Add stock or water and bring to a rapid boil. Adjust heat to a low simmer and cook uncovered for 45 minutes, but begin checking after 30 minutes. Rice should not be too soft. Rice may be done before all liquid is absorbed. Place a clean, thin towel or cheesecloth inside a colander and drain. Transfer drained rice to a serving bowl.

Combine remaining ingredients and toss thoroughly. Let the mixture stand for at least 2 hours to blend flavors. Pour mixture over rice in serving bowl. If making ahead of time, store in refrigerator. Bring to room temperature for serving. Garnish with mint leaves.

Cranberry Sauce à la Jennifer

Yield: 5 cups

2 12 ounce packages fresh cranberries
3 1/3 cups sugar
1 1/2 cups coarsely chopped, toasted walnuts (approximately 6 ounces)
1/4 cup orange liqueur
fresh lemon juice, optional

Preheat oven to 350 degrees. Rinse and drain cranberries. Place in a 15x10x2 glass baking dish. Stir in sugar. Cover with foil. Bake until cranberries burst and sauce begins to thicken; stirring every 20 minutes for a total of 1 hour 15 minutes. Cool completely. Stir in walnuts and orange liqueur, add lemon juice to taste, if desired. Transfer to a bowl. Cover and refrigerate.

Hint: Can prepare up to two days ahead.

Black Bean, Roasted Corn & Avocado Salad on a Bed of Red Quinoa

1 cup red quinoa
2 cups chicken or vegetable broth
1 15 ounce can black beans, drained and rinsed
2 cups corn kernels, roasted
1 avocado, cut into 1/2 inch pieces
1 pint grape tomatoes, halved
1/2 cup finely diced red onion
3/4 cup cilantro salad dressing
sea salt and pepper, to taste
zest of lime
1/2 bunch cilantro, chopped, divided
1/4 cup olive oil

Cook quinoa with broth according to package directions. While quinoa is cooking, combine beans, corn, avocado, tomatoes and onion. Top with salad dressing; toss gently. Add salt, pepper and lime zest, to taste. Add 1/2 of cilantro; gently toss once more. Set aside. When quinoa is cooked, toss with olive oil; add salt and pepper to taste. Set aside to cool. When ready to serve, spread quinoa on a large serving platter; top with corn and bean mixture. Garnish with remaining cilantro.

Vegetarian Chili

2 tablespoons olive oil
2 large onions, chopped
4 large garlic cloves, chopped
2 jalapeño chilis, minced
2 28 ounce cans crushed tomatoes
1 6 ounce can tomato paste
2 green bell peppers, chopped
2 large carrots, chopped
1 tablespoon ground cumin
3/4 teaspoon salt
1/2 teaspoon cayenne pepper
2 15 ounce cans kidney beans, drained
2 15 ounce cans pinto beans, drained
2 small zucchini, diced
grated Cheddar cheese, garnish
chopped onion, garnish

Heat oil in heavy large pot. Add onions, garlic and chilis. For more "fire" include the chili seeds. Sauté until onions are translucent, about 6 minutes. Add tomatoes, tomato paste, bell peppers, carrots, cumin, salt and cayenne pepper. Bring to simmer. Cook for 20 minutes. Add all beans; cook 15 minutes. Add zucchini; cook 5 minutes. Ladle into bowls. Serve cheese and chopped onion separately.

Pasta

Pasta

Baked Macaroni and Cheese

Yield: Serves 6

2 cups elbow macaroni, uncooked
1/2 cup butter
1/2 cup flour
1 1/2 cups milk
1 1/2 cups sour cream
1 teaspoon salt
1/2 teaspoon pepper
1 10 ounce bar mild Cheddar cheese, grated, divided

Preheat oven to 350 degrees. Cook macaroni in salted boiling water, according to package directions. Drain and rinse with cold water. Pour into a 3 quart casserole. In a saucepan, melt butter and stir in flour. Gradually stir in milk and sour cream. Add salt and pepper. Cook over low heat, stirring constantly, until sauce bubbles and thickens. Reserve 1 cup grated cheese for the top of casserole. Toss macaroni with remaining cheese. Pour sauce over macaroni and mix thoroughly. Sprinkle with reserved cheese. Bake for 1 hour, or until bubbly and brown. Serve immediately.

3-Cheese Macaroni

Yield: Serves 8-10

2 3/4 cups macaroni (12 ounces)
cooking spray
1 1/2 cups milk
1/4 cup butter, melted
1/2 teaspoon white pepper
1/4 teaspoon salt
8 ounces jack, Muenster or mozzarella cheese, shredded
2 cups shredded Cheddar cheese
1 8 ounce package cream cheese, cubed

Preheat oven to 350 degrees. Cook macaroni and put in casserole greased with cooking spray Add milk, butter, pepper and salt. Stir in cheeses. Bake uncovered for 20 minutes. Let stand for 10 minutes.

Grandma Eliza's Macaroni and Cheese

1 16 ounce package macaroni
1 1/2 teaspoons salt, divided
3 tablespoons canola oil, divided
1 cup crumbled feta cheese
2 cups grated Parmesan cheese, divided
6 eggs, beaten
1/4 teaspoon white pepper, to taste
1 1/2 cups milk

Boil macaroni according to directions, adding 1 teaspoon salt and 1 tablespoon oil in water. Drain and rinse in a colander. Place macaroni in a large bowl; add feta cheese and 1 cup of Parmesan cheese; mix thoroughly. Preheat oven to 350 degrees and spray or grease two 9x13 inch pans. In bowl, place eggs, 1/2 teaspoon salt, pepper, milk and 2 tablespoons oil. Mix well and add to macaroni mixture. Fill pans with mixture. Sprinkle tops with remaining cup of Parmesan cheese. Bake for 30 minutes or until golden brown.

Hint: One pan may be frozen for future use.

Greek Orzo

1 medium onion, chopped fine
2 tablespoons olive oil, divided
1 cup orzo
3 cups water, approximately
1 8 ounce can tomato sauce or 3 tablespoons tomato paste
salt and pepper, to taste

In a large frying pan that has a lid, sauté onion in 1 tablespoon olive oil until browned. Add another 1 tablespoon olive oil and orzo; sauté until orzo browns slightly. Don't let it burn. Add 2 cups water and tomato sauce or tomato paste. Stir well. Turn heat down, cover and cook, checking after 10 minutes. Stir, add more water as needed, and continue cooking until pasta is soft. Season with salt and pepper.

Kasha Varnishkes (Buckwheat and Bow-Tie Noodles)

Yield: Serves 8-10

2 large onions, finely chopped
4 to 6 tablespoons vegetable oil or chicken fat
1 1/2 cups sliced mushrooms
1 13 ounce box kasha (roasted large-size buckwheat)
1 teaspoon salt or garlic salt
1/2 teaspoon pepper or seasoned pepper
1/2 teaspoon paprika
1 to 2 eggs, beaten
2 1/2 to 3 cups boiling beef broth, bouillon or water
1 8 ounce package bow-tie noodles or 1/2 16 ounce package bow-tie noodles
1 1/2 to 2 tablespoons pareve margarine

In a large skillet (with tight fitting lid), sauté onions in oil or chicken fat until brown. Add mushrooms and sauté a few minutes longer. Stir in kasha, salt, pepper, paprika and eggs. Continue to stir until mixture looks dry. Then turn kasha into large pot to accommodate liquid. Add liquid slowly. Turn heat lower so that kasha will simmer. Cover and cook for about 10 minutes, or until liquid is absorbed. Cook bow-tie noodles as directed on package, drain and return to pot. Add margarine to noodles and stir until coated. Add noodles to kasha mixture. Check for salt and pepper. If kasha is too dry, add a little broth. Put kasha mixture in casserole and cover tightly with lid or aluminum foil. Bake in 350 degree oven for 25 to 30 minutes, or until thoroughly heated. Kasha can be heated in the microwave oven in a heatproof casserole, covered with plastic wrap, cooked on high 3 to 4 minutes. Stir with fork, cover again and heat for another 1 to 2 minutes or until fully heated.

Hint: Kasha may be made a day ahead. Bring to room temperature and reheat.

Angel Hair Pasta, Tomatoes and Goat Cheese

Yield: Serves 2-4

3 tablespoons olive oil, divided
2 cloves garlic, minced
1 15 ounce can diced tomatoes
1 teaspoon dried basil
1/2 teaspoon dried oregano
1/2 pound angel hair pasta (capellini)
salt
4 ounces goat cheese
1/4 heaping teaspoon red pepper flakes, garnish

In a pot, heat 2 tablespoons olive oil over medium heat. Sauté garlic for 1 minute. Add diced tomatoes with juice and dried herbs. Cover; simmer 10 minutes. Bring a large pot of salted water to a boil. Add pasta and boil, uncovered, until al dente. Angel hair cooks fast, do not overcook. Drain, put back in pot and drizzle 1 tablespoon olive oil over pasta, toss to keep from sticking. To serve, divide pasta into bowls, top with a little sauce and some goat cheese, stir lightly. Top with red pepper flakes to taste.

Dairy Spaghetti – A Dad's and Kid's Quick Dish!

1/4 pound butter or margarine
1 16 ounce package spaghetti
8 ounces milk
1 8 ounce can tomato sauce
1 8 ounce package (or more) sharp Cheddar cheese, grated, divided
4 ounces (or more) Parmesan cheese, grated, divided

Melt butter or margarine in 9x13 casserole dish. Boil spaghetti until tender; drain. Pour into baking dish. Add milk and tomato sauce. Use a fork to mix thoroughly. Add 3/4 package of sharp Cheddar; mix into casserole mixture. Add 2 ounces Parmesan cheese; mix into casserole mixture. Use remaining cheeses to cover top of casserole. Bake uncovered at 350 degrees until top is golden brown.

Variation: For a dish that will appeal to adults: add Kalamata olives, onion, fresh tomatoes, basil and sliced smoked mozzarella on top.

Italian Pasta

2 red bell peppers, cored, seeded, cut into 1-inch strips
2 zucchini, quartered lengthwise, cut into 1-inch strips
2 summer squash, quartered lengthwise, cut into 1-inch pieces
4 crimini mushrooms, quartered
1 yellow onion, sliced into 1-inch strips
1/4 cup extra virgin olive oil
1 teaspoon salt, divided
1/2 teaspoon freshly ground pepper, divided
1 tablespoon herbs de Provence
1 pound penne pasta
3 cups marinara sauce
1 cup grated fontina cheese
1/2 cup grated smoked mozzarella
1/4 cup grated Parmesan cheese, plus 1/3 cup for topping
1 1/2 cups frozen peas, thawed
2 tablespoons unsalted butter, cut into small pieces

Preheat oven to 450 degrees. On a baking sheet, toss bell peppers, zucchini, squash, mushrooms and onion with olive oil, 1/2 teaspoon salt, 1/4 teaspoon pepper and herbs. Bake until tender, about 15 minutes. Bring a large pot of salted water to a boil over high heat. Add pasta and cook for about 6 minutes. Since you will be cooking pasta a second time in oven, make sure it is not completely cooked. Drain in colander. In a large bowl, combine pasta with roasted vegetables, marinara sauce, fontina, mozzarella, 1/4 cup Parmesan, peas, remaining 1/2 teaspoon salt and 1/4 teaspoon pepper. Gently mix, using a wooden spoon, until all pasta is coated with sauce and ingredients are combined. Pour pasta into a greased 9x13 baking dish. Top with remaining 1/3 cup Parmesan cheese and butter pieces. Bake until top is golden and cheese melts, about 25 minutes.

La Mein

1 8 ounce box fine egg noodles
vegetable oil to cover bottom of pan
1 package dry onion soup mix
1 cup raw rice
3 cups boiling water
garlic powder, to taste
soy sauce, to taste

Brown egg noodles in oil. Stir continuously, until golden brown. Add all other ingredients, stirring well. Cover and cook on low heat for about 30 minutes.

Variation: Can add chicken or vegetables.

Luci's Pasta

6 tablespoons olive oil, divided
1 medium onion, chopped
1 teaspoon garlic, minced
3 28 ounce cans plum tomatoes with basil, drained
1 teaspoon dried basil
1 teaspoon dried, crushed red pepper
2 cups canned low-salt vegetable broth
salt and pepper
1 pound penne
2 1/2 cups shredded Havarti
1/2 cup grated Parmesan cheese
1/3 cup black olives, sliced

Heat 3 tablespoons olive oil; sauté onions and garlic until translucent (5 minutes). Mix in drained tomatoes, basil and crushed red pepper; bring to a boil. Break up tomatoes with back of a spoon. Add broth, simmer for 1 hour and 10 minutes. Stir occasionally while simmering (should reduce to 6 cups). When finished, season with salt and pepper, to taste. Cook penne according to package instructions, drain. Preheat oven to 375 degrees. Toss cooked pasta with 3 tablespoons olive oil, sauce, cheeses and olives. Bake for 30 minutes.

Ziti with Tuna, Capers and Raisins

Yield: Serves 2-4

1/2 pound ziti (or penne)
2 tablespoons olive oil, divided
1 carrot, coarsely chopped
1 stalk celery, coarsely chopped
1/4 cup chopped flat-leaf parsley
3 tablespoons capers, drained
3 tablespoons golden raisins
1 teaspoon salt
1/2 onion, chopped, optional
1/4 teaspoon red pepper flakes, optional
1 6 ounce can solid white tuna, drained and flaked
1 teaspoon dried basil
1/4 teaspoon dried oregano
Parmesan cheese, to taste
3 tablespoons pine nuts, optional

Bring a large pot of salted water to a boil, add pasta; boil uncovered until al dente. Before draining, save about 1 cup pasta water. Drain. Heat 1 tablespoon olive oil in large frying pan, sauté carrots, celery, parsley, capers, raisins, salt, optional onion and red pepper flakes over medium heat for 7 minutes. Set aside. In a small bowl, mix drained tuna with dried herbs and 1 tablespoon olive oil. In a large serving bowl, mix pasta, vegetable mixture, tuna and a little pasta cooking water to moisten. Top with Parmesan cheese and pine nuts.

Spaghetti with Tuna and Lemon

2 tablespoons olive oil
1 clove garlic, finely chopped
4 tablespoons chopped parsley
7 ounce can albacore tuna, drained and flaked
1 pound spaghetti
juice of 1 lemon
3/4 cup freshly grated Parmesan cheese
2 tablespoons butter, in small pieces
salt and freshly ground black pepper, to taste

Heat olive oil; add garlic and parsley. Stir continually over low heat, gradually adding tuna. Heat should remain low, so that none of ingredients changes color. Cook pasta, following the packet directions carefully to avoid overcooking. Drain pasta and turn into a heated serving dish. Add sauce and stir well. Add lemon juice, Parmesan cheese, butter, salt and black pepper. Stir well and serve at once.

Variation: Another more strongly-flavored version of this sauce can be made leaving out the cheese and butter, adding 3 chopped anchovy fillets and 1/2 small minced chili pepper to the initial frying of garlic and parsley.

Judy's Israeli Couscous

Yield: Serves 20

2 1/2 pounds Israeli couscous (larger pearls)
1/2 cup chopped parsley
1/2 cup finely chopped red onion
1 cup minced dried apricots
1/2 cup dried cranberries
1/2 cup vegetable oil
1 cup white balsamic vinegar
1/4 cup chopped fresh mint
1/2 cup fresh lemon juice
salt and pepper, to taste
1/4 cup sliced, toasted almonds, garnish
1/4 cup chopped green onion, garnish

In a sauce pot, bring 7 cups water and 1 tablespoon salt to a boil. Stir in couscous, cover and take off heat. Let stand for at least 30 minutes. Fluff with fork and spread evenly on a sheet pan; refrigerate until cool. Mix cooled couscous with all ingredients, except salt, pepper, almonds and green onions, in a mixing bowl. Gently toss and season with salt and pepper. Garnish with almonds and green onions.

Note: It may be halved.

Bow-Ties with Creamy Fennel, Broccoli and Spinach Sauce

1 small fresh fennel bulb (about 1/2 pound), stalks and leaves discarded
1 pound broccoli stalks, peeled and cut into 1-inch pieces
2 cups packed fresh spinach leaves, stemmed and rinsed well in cold water, but not dried
1 tablespoon olive oil
kosher salt
freshly ground black pepper
1/2 pound dry bow-tie noodles

Cut fennel bulb into 1-inch pieces. Combine fennel and broccoli in a small saucepan, with just enough water to cover. Bring to a boil over medium-high heat; turn heat to low and simmer about 10 minutes until fennel is tender. Add spinach; stir to combine. Cook 1 minute until spinach is wilted and tender. Drain vegetables, reserving cooking liquid. Place vegetables in container of a processor or blender; process about 30 seconds until smooth. Add liquid, 1/4 cup at a time, until purée is consistency of a thick soup. Add olive oil; process about 10 seconds. Season with salt and pepper, to taste. Transfer purée to saucepan. Reheat before serving. Bring a large pot of water to a rolling boil over high heat. Add bow-tie noodles. Cook, stirring occasionally, 7 to 10 minutes until the pasta is tender but firm, al dente. Drain; transfer to a large, preheated serving bowl. Add fennel and broccoli sauce; toss well before serving.

Variation: For a more substantial dish, add some cooked broccoli florets to the finished dish.

Orzo, Spinach, Feta Salad

1 pound orzo pasta
16 ounces (full bottle) Greek salad dressing with feta
1 12 ounce bag washed fresh spinach
1 6 ounce jar sun-dried tomatoes, diced
1 8 ounce package feta cheese chunks
1 small jar pitted Kalamata olives
3 garlic cloves, diced
1/2 cup fresh lemon juice
2 tablespoons olive oil

Prepare orzo as directed on the package. Place in a large bowl and add 3/4 of the salad dressing. Stir until well coated. Add remaining ingredients. Toss well with remaining salad dressing. Serve.

Pasta Salad with Herb Pesto and Peas

Yield: Serves 8

salt, divided
1 pound tricolor short, curly pasta or campanelle
1/4 cup pine nuts
1/2 cup flat-leaf parsley
20 to 25 fresh basil leaves (about 1 cup)
6 sprigs of fresh tarragon, leaves stripped from stems
1/2 cup freshly grated Parmigiano-Reggiano cheese
1 garlic clove, peeled
juice of 1 lemon
1/3 to 1/2 cup extra-virgin olive oil
freshly ground pepper
1 10 ounce box frozen peas, thawed
1/2 red bell pepper, finely chopped
4 small celery ribs from the heart, finely chopped with leaves
4 scallions, thinly sliced at an angle

Bring a large pot of water to a boil. Salt water, add pasta and cook until al dente. Toast pine nuts in a small skillet over low heat, shaking pan occasionally, until golden, about 3 minutes; let cool. In a food processor, pulse to chop toasted pine nuts, parsley, basil, tarragon, cheese, garlic and lemon juice. Slowly pour in 1/3 cup olive oil, while food processor is running. Process until a thick pesto forms; add remaining olive oil, if needed. Season to taste with salt and pepper; pulse again to incorporate. Place pesto in a large, shallow serving dish. Add peas and red bell pepper. When pasta is almost cooked, add a ladle of its starchy cooking water to pesto and mix. Drain pasta well. Stir celery and scallions into sauce, add pasta and toss to coat. Adjust seasonings to taste.

Kugels and Casseroles

Kugels and Casseroles

Apricot Kugel

1 12 ounce package wide noodles
4 ounces margarine
6 eggs
8 ounces light sour cream
16 ounces low-fat cottage cheese
1/2 cup sugar
1/2 cup low-fat milk
1/2 cup golden raisins
8 ounces dried apricots, cut up

TOPPING
1 cup corn flakes
1 cup golden brown sugar
4 ounces margarine, softened

In large pot, cook noodles until tender. Drain, return to pot; add margarine. Mix until margarine is melted. Set aside. In large bowl, beat eggs. Add sour cream, cottage cheese, sugar and milk to beaten eggs. Mix well. Add dry fruit. Combine with noodles in large pot. Pour into greased 9x13 glass ovenproof baking dish or aluminum pan. In medium bowl, mix corn flakes, brown sugar and margarine. With spoon, sprinkle small blobs of topping over entire kugel batter. Bake at 350 degrees for 1 hour. Cut when cool. Kugel may be frozen and then reheated, covered with aluminum foil. May also be reheated in microwave oven, covered with plastic wrap.

Honey Apple Noodle Kugel

1 12 ounce package medium noodles
6 eggs
1/2 cup sugar
1 teaspoon cinnamon
1 19 ounce can apple pie filling
1 cup raisins
1 tablespoon oil
1/2 cup honey
2 teaspoons lemon juice

Boil noodles until soft; drain. Beat eggs. Add sugar, cinnamon, apple pie filling and raisins. Heat oil in bottom of a 9x12 glass ovenproof baking dish. Add noodles to egg mixture and pour into hot pan. Bake at 300 degrees for 30 minutes. Mix together honey and lemon juice. Pour over kugel and bake for 45 minutes. Allow to cool and cut in squares when cold. Reheat to serve.

Delicious sweet way to start off a New Year. My mother made this recipe for years, then I made it for years and now my daughters make it.

Aunt Silvia's Famous Noodle Pudding

Yield: Serves 15-20

PUDDING

1 pound broad noodles
1 pound cottage cheese
1 cup white raisins
1 1/2 teaspoons vanilla
1/2 teaspoon salt
1/4 pound melted butter
7 eggs, beaten
3 cups milk
1 pint sour cream
1/2 cup sugar

TOPPING

1/2 cup crushed corn flakes
1 teaspoon cinnamon
1 teaspoon sugar
butter

Combine pudding ingredients in large bowl. Mix well. Pour into large pan and refrigerate overnight (consistency will be loose). When ready to bake, mix corn flakes, cinnamon and sugar together in a small bowl; sprinkle over pudding. Dot top with butter. Bake at 350 degrees for 1 1/2 hours or until golden brown.

Pareve Noodle Kugel

16 ounces wide egg noodles
1/4 pound pareve margarine, melted
8 eggs
3 cups orange juice plus pulp of 1 orange
1 teaspoon salt
2 tart apples, grated
2 teaspoons lemon juice
1 teaspoon vanilla
1 tablespoon cinnamon
1 cup sugar

Cook noodles and toss with melted margarine. Beat eggs, orange juice, pulp of orange and salt. Pour over noodles. Mix grated apples, lemon juice and vanilla; add to noodles and mix. Pour into 9x13 greased pan. Sprinkle top with cinnamon and sugar. Bake in 350 degree oven for 1 hour.

Mushroom Kugel

2 large onions, diced or 1 package frozen chopped onions, thawed
5 tablespoons vegetable oil, divided
1 can mushrooms, stems and pieces or 1 package sliced fresh mushrooms
1 16 ounce package wide noodles
3 eggs
1 tablespoon baking powder
1/2 teaspoon salt
1 teaspoon sugar
dash pepper
1 cup chicken soup or 1/2 teaspoon instant chicken soup mix added to the mushroom juice and water to make 1 cup

Fry onions in 2 tablespoons oil; when half done, add drained mushrooms (save liquid) or fresh mushrooms. Fry until onions are light brown. Boil noodles and drain. Return noodles to pot; add 3 tablespoons oil. Combine beaten eggs with rest of ingredients; add to noodle mixture. Pour into greased glass ovenproof dish or aluminum 9x13 pan. Bake 1 hour at 350 degrees. Cool and cut into 24 pieces. Can be frozen and reheated, covered with aluminum foil.

Noodle Kugel

4 eggs
1 cup orange juice
3/4 cup sugar
1 cup sour cream
8 ounces cream cheese, softened
1 pound wide noodles
1 stick margarine, melted

Beat eggs. Mix in orange juice. Add sugar, sour cream and cream cheese. Cook noodles, according to package directions. Add margarine to noodles. Add egg mixture to noodles. Place noodles, mixed with everything from above, in an ovenproof dish.

TOPPING
1 cup crushed corn flakes
1 cup brown sugar
1/4 cup margarine, melted

Mix topping ingredients together and put on top of unbaked noodles. Bake at 325 degrees for 1 to 1 1/2 hours.

Spinach Noodle Kugel

5 drops oil
1 pound package wide noodles
2 to 3 medium onions, chopped
2 sticks butter or margarine, divided
4 eggs, beaten
2 packages frozen chopped spinach, thawed and squeezed dry
1 pint sour cream
1 1/2 cups shredded Gruyere cheese
1 tablespoon seasoned salt
cooking spray

Add oil to water and boil noodles. Drain when done. Sauté onions in 1 stick butter or margarine until soft and golden. Mix eggs, spinach, sour cream and cheese until well-blended. Melt 1 stick butter or margarine; mix with noodles. Combine all ingredients; add salt. Lightly coat Bundt pan with cooking spray. Pour mixture into Bundt pan. Bake at 350 degrees for 1 1/4 hours or until done. Turn upside down on plate.

Pecan Crunch Kugel

1/2 pound wide noodles
salt
1/2 cup butter
6 eggs
1 cup sour cream
1 cup cottage cheese
1/2 cup sugar
1/2 cup milk

TOPPING

1/2 cup crushed corn flakes
1 1/2 cups brown sugar
3/8 cup melted butter
1/4 to 1/2 cup (or more) chopped pecans

Boil noodles in salted water. Drain; melt butter in hot noodles, coating noodles well. Cool noodles slightly. Beat together eggs, sour cream, cottage cheese, sugar and milk. Add to cooled noodles. Place in greased 9x13 glass ovenproof pan. Top with topping made from remaining ingredients. Bake 1 hour at 350 degrees. Can be made ahead and reheated.

Chili Rellenos Casserole

Yield: Serves 8-10

1 27 ounce can whole roasted green chilies
1 1/2 pounds jack cheese, grated
1 1/2 pounds Cheddar cheese, grated
5 eggs
3 tablespoons flour
1 12 ounce can evaporated milk
1 15 ounce can tomato sauce

Wash chilies, after cutting them open, remove seeds. Pat dry all chilies. In a 9x13 baking dish, layer half the chilies, then half the two cheeses over the chilies. Make another layer of chilies and cheese, but save 1/2 cup of cheese for topping. Beat eggs, flour and evaporated milk until blended. Pour egg mixture over chilies and cheese. Casserole can be refrigerated at this point, if desired. Bake at 350 degrees for 30 minutes. Spread tomato sauce over top. Sprinkle with reserved cheese; bake 15 to 20 minutes longer. Remove from oven; let cheese set for 5 to 10 minutes, then cut into squares and serve.

Corn, Chili and Cheese Casserole

Yield: Serves 15-20, as a side dish

2 14 to 15 ounce cans cream-style corn
1 11 ounce can regular corn
2 4 ounce cans diced green chilies
1 cup melted butter
4 eggs, beaten
1 cup cornmeal
2 cups sour cream
4 cups diced Monterey Jack cheese
1 teaspoon salt

Preheat oven to 375 degrees. Mix together all ingredients in a large bowl. Place into a well-greased 9x13 baking dish (pan will be full, but shouldn't overflow). Bake casserole for 50 minutes or until mixture is set.

Note: This recipe can be assembled the day before and refrigerated overnight, then baked the following day.

Cheese Enchilada Casserole

1 32 ounce can enchilada sauce
1 36 count bag corn tortillas, (you will have left-overs)
1 15 to 20 ounce can corn, drained, but not rinsed
1 15 to 20 ounce can black beans, drained, but not rinsed
1 to 2 bags shredded Mexican cheese blend (2 to 4 cups)

Preheat oven to 350 degrees. Use a 9x12 pan or any pan of that approximate size. Begin with a layer of enchilada sauce on bottom of pan. Add a layer of tortillas (overlapping tortillas a bit works best). Add corn and black beans. Cover with more sauce and top with cheese. Repeat for 3 layers. On top of last layer, add a layer of tortillas and cover with sauce to keep it moist. Cover and bake for 15 minutes; uncover and bake until bubbling and a bit golden.

Note: You may want to use more beans, corn or anything else you want to throw in the mix, so have extra on hand.

Barley Vegetable Casserole

Yield: Serves 4

2/3 cup barley
water
cooking spray
1 cup onion, chopped
oil
1 cup mushrooms, chopped
1 cup carrots, finely shredded
1 cup cauliflower florets, chopped into 1/4 inch pieces
2 1/2 cups vegetable broth
1/4 teaspoon garlic powder
salt and pepper

Preheat oven to 350 degrees. Place barley and small amount of water in a heavy nonstick skillet over medium heat. Cook 2 to 3 minutes, stirring frequently, until lightly browned. Transfer to a casserole dish that has been lightly coated with cooking spray. Sauté onions in a small amount of oil for 5 minutes in same skillet, stirring frequently. Combine onions with remaining vegetables and add to casserole. Combine vegetable broth and garlic powder in a bowl. Mix well and stir into casserole. Season with salt and pepper, to taste; mix well. Cover; bake 1 1/4 hours, until barley is tender and most of liquid has been absorbed. Stir several times while baking. Let stand 5 minutes, mix and serve.

Claire's Egg and Spinach Casserole

Yield: Serves 6-8

vegetable or canola oil
1/4 cup butter
1 onion, minced
5 eggs, beaten
1 16 ounce package frozen, chopped spinach, thawed and squeezed dry
1 16 ounce carton cottage cheese
1 1/2 cups shredded Cheddar cheese
3 tablespoons flour
2 dashes Worcestershire sauce
1 tablespoon dried dill
salt and pepper, to taste

Preheat oven to 350 degrees. Oil a 9x13 glass baking dish. Melt butter in frying pan; sauté onions until soft and golden. In a large bowl, combine beaten eggs and spinach. Mix in cottage cheese, Cheddar cheese, flour, Worcestershire sauce, dill, salt and pepper. Add onions and stir well. Pour into prepared baking dish; bake 40 to 45 minutes, until top is golden and mixture is set.

Variation: Can be made with zucchini or other vegetables.

Cantor's Concert Eggplant, Tomato and Pesto Casserole

Yield: Serves 15

EGGPLANT
3 1/2 eggplants
olive oil

Preheat oven to 400 degrees. Cut ends off eggplants and slice crosswise into 1/4 to 3/8 inch slices. Cover 2 baking sheets with heavy aluminum foil. Brush foil generously with olive oil. Arrange eggplant slices, close together in a single layer; brush with olive oil. Bake for 12 minutes, rotate pans and bake for 15 to 17 minutes or until eggplants are soft and bottom of eggplants are a light brown. Remove from oven and loosen from foil. Cool.

(Recipe continued on next page)

Cantor's Concert Eggplant, Tomato and Pesto Casserole *(continued)*

TOMATO SAUCE

- 1/3 cup olive oil
- 2 medium onions, chopped
- 1/3 cup diced sun-dried tomatoes
- 1 cup water
- 1 28 ounce can Italian plum tomatoes
- 1/2 pound zucchini, sliced very thin
- 1 1/2 teaspoons dried oregano
- 1 tablespoon raspberry or wine vinegar
- salt and pepper to taste

In a large frying pan, heat olive oil, add onions and sauté for about 2 minutes. Cover pan with sheet of wax paper and a lid; cook over low heat, stirring occasionally, until onion is soft but not brown, about 8 to 10 minutes. While onions are cooking, place sun-dried tomatoes in 2 cup measure, with water, cover with plastic wrap and microwave on high for 3 to 4 minutes. Remove tomatoes and put in food processor with metal blade, add 1/4 cup of liquid; process until puréed. Cut canned tomatoes in half, squeeze out seeds and cut off hard stems. Add to food processor and pulse until chunky. Stir into onions. Add zucchini, oregano, vinegar, salt and pepper. Cook, uncovered, over moderate heat, stirring occasionally, until zucchini is soft, 5 to 7 minutes.

PESTO

- 3 large cloves garlic
- 1 cup fresh basil, lightly packed
- 1 cup Italian parsley
- 1/4 cup shredded Parmesan cheese
- 1/2 cup toasted pine nuts
- 1 1/2 tablespoons water
- 1 1/2 tablespoons olive oil

In food processor with metal blade, mince garlic, basil, Italian parsley, Parmesan cheese and nuts. Process until ground. Add water and olive oil. Pulse until blended.

CASSEROLE

- olive oil
- 1 cup dry bread crumbs
- 6 ounces sliced mozzarella cheese
- 3 tablespoons shredded Parmesan cheese

Grease or spray with olive oil a 9-inch springform pan. Sprinkle bread crumbs over bottom. Spoon 1 cup tomato sauce over bread crumbs; sauce will not cover bread crumbs. Arrange 1/3 eggplant over sauce. Spread with 1 cup tomato sauce, layer with half sliced cheese, half pesto, 1/3 eggplant, 1 cup tomato sauce, remaining cheese, pesto, eggplant and tomato sauce. Wrap springform bottom in heavy aluminum foil and place on baking sheet. Bake, covered with aluminum foil, in center of oven until heated through, about 45 minutes. Bring to room temperature, 50 to 60 minutes. Sprinkle with Parmesan cheese and bake, uncovered, for 10 minutes. Let stand 15 minutes before serving or cool and refrigerate, covered, overnight. To reheat, bring to room temperature and bake, uncovered, at 400 degrees for 17 to 20 minutes or until heated through.

Desserts

Desserts

Desserts (continued)

Best Ever Brownie, Marshmallow and Crispy Rice Bar Cookies

1 box brownie mix
1 tablespoon butter
1 3/4 cups chocolate chips
1 cup peanut butter
1 3/4 cups crisped rice cereal
10 ounces mini marshmallows

Make brownie mix according to directions on box. Put brownie batter into well-greased 9x13 baking dish (be sure to grease sides of pan). Bake according to instructions on back of box for a 9x13 dish.

While brownies are baking, melt butter, chocolate chips and peanut butter together in a saucepan. Add cereal to chocolate mixture; stir. Remove baked brownies from oven; spread mini-marshmallows over top of hot brownies. Put pan with brownies and marshmallows back into oven for 3 to 5 minutes, or until marshmallows have puffed up a bit. Remove brownies and marshmallows from oven; spread chocolate mixture over top. Allow entire pan to cool completely; cut into bars. (You will most likely need to put pan into refrigerator to cool for at least 1 hour before cutting bars.)

Chocolate Bar Cookies

1 cup margarine or butter
3/4 cup sugar
1 egg
1/2 teaspoon salt, optional
2 1/2 cups flour
2 teaspoons vanilla
3 8 ounce milk chocolate bars, with or without almonds

Cream margarine and sugar. Add other ingredients, except chocolate bars. Mix. Put 1/2 of dough in a 9x13 ungreased pan. Press down to cover bottom of dish. Place chocolate bars side by side on dough. Press other half of dough to cover bars. Bake at 350 degrees for 20 minutes. Cool several hours. Cut on the diagonal.

Magic Cookie Bars

1 stick unsalted butter, melted
1 1/2 cups graham cracker crumbs
1 can sweetened condensed milk
1 6 ounce package semi-sweet chocolate chips
4 ounces sweetened coconut
1 cup chopped walnuts

Pour melted butter in a 13×9 inch pan. Layer (in order) graham cracker crumbs, milk, chocolate chips, coconut and nuts. Press down gently. Bake at 350 degrees (325 degrees for glass pan) for 30 minutes or until lightly browned.

Pumpkin and Chocolate Chip Brownie Bar Cookies

2 cups all-purpose flour
1 teaspoon baking soda
3/4 teaspoon salt
2 teaspoons cinnamon
1 teaspoon ground ginger
1/4 teaspoon ground nutmeg
1/8 teaspoon ground allspice
1/8 teaspoon ground cloves
1 cup butter, room temperature
1 1/4 cups sugar
1 large egg
2 teaspoons vanilla
1 cup canned pumpkin
1 1/2 cups chocolate chips

Preheat oven to 350 degrees. Line bottom of 9x13 baking dish with aluminum foil, leaving an overhang on all four sides. Combine flour, baking soda, salt and spices; set aside. Cream butter and sugar until smooth. Add egg and vanilla; mix until combined. Add pumpkin, scraping down sides of bowl. Mixture may appear separated. Lower speed on mixer; add dry ingredients, until just combined. Fold in chocolate chips by hand; spread batter into prepared pan. Bake 40 to 45 minutes until edges pull away from sides and only some small moist crumbs stick to tester stick. Cool in pan. Use aluminum foil sides to lift brownies from pan. Use a serrated knife to cut into squares.

Vanilla Bean Almond Cookie Bars

1/2 cup melted butter
1/2 cup brown sugar
1/4 cup granulated sugar
1 package almond paste
1 bourbon Madagascar vanilla bean
2 teaspoons vanilla extract
1 large egg
2 cups whole-wheat pastry flour
1/2 cup all-purpose flour
1/4 teaspoon baking soda
2 tablespoons almond liqueur or 2 teaspoons almond extract

Preheat oven to 350 degrees. Cream butter and sugars together. Grate almond paste with big-hole side of cheese grater. Add vanilla bean by cutting in half and gliding a knife down center to get bean seeds, then add vanilla extract. Add egg, pastry flour, all-purpose flour and baking soda. Add almond liqueur or almond extract. Mix well. Spread evenly on a sprayed 13x9x2 metal baking pan. Bake for 10 to 15 minutes or until a light golden hue. Let cool completely in pan over wire rack.

Flourless Chocolate Cookies

1/2 pound bittersweet chocolate
3 tablespoons butter or margarine, room temperature
2 eggs
1/3 cup sugar, plus more for rolling
1/2 cup finely ground almonds
parchment paper
confectioners sugar

Melt chocolate, in top of double boiler set over, but not touching, simmering water. Remove from heat. Cut butter into a few pieces and mix into chocolate until melted. Beat eggs with electric mixer, gradually adding the sugar until ribbon forms, approximately 10 minutes. Fold into butter/chocolate mixture. Gently add ground almonds. Cover and refrigerate overnight. Preheat oven to 325 degrees. Line baking sheet with parchment paper. Use a cookie scoop to form 1 inch balls. Roll balls in granulated sugar. Place on baking sheet about 2-inches apart and immediately place in oven. Bake until center of cookies are no longer wet, 9 to 13 minutes. When slightly cool, lightly dust with confectioners sugar.

Note: These cookies can be made dairy, pareve or for Passover.

Linda's Peanut Butter Cookies

1/2 cup margarine or butter
1/2 cup granulated sugar
1/2 cup brown sugar, packed
1 egg
3/4 to 1 cup old-fashioned chunky peanut butter
1 1/8 cups sifted flour
1 teaspoon baking soda
1 teaspoon vanilla

Blend margarine and sugars. Add egg; mix. Add peanut butter; mix. Add flour and baking soda; mix. Add vanilla; mix. Make batter into round balls and place on cookie sheet. Preheat oven to 375 degrees. Bake for 8 to 10 minutes. Watch carefully. When cookies start to crack on top, remove from oven. Be careful cookies don't burn on bottom.

Variation: Add 1/2 cup chocolate chips.

Oatmeal Crispies

1 cup butter
1 cup brown sugar, packed
1 cup sugar
2 eggs, beaten
1 teaspoon vanilla
1 1/2 cups flour
1 teaspoon salt
1 teaspoon baking soda
3 cups rolled oats
1/2 cup chopped walnuts or pecans, optional

Thoroughly cream butter and sugars. Add eggs and vanilla. Add all remaining ingredients; blend well. Shape mixture into 3 rolls, wrap in plastic, chill 1 hour or freeze. Slice 1/4 inch thick. Bake on ungreased cookie sheets in 350 degree oven for 15 minutes or until lightly browned. Cookies will crisp as they cool.

Note: These can be dropped by teaspoons, instead of slicing, they will spread a lot.

Pumpkin Chocolate Chip Cookies

1/4 cup unbleached all-purpose flour
1 cup whole-wheat pastry flour
1/4 cup granulated sugar
1/2 cup brown sugar
1 teaspoon ground cinnamon
1 teaspoon ground ginger
1/4 teaspoon ground cloves
1/4 teaspoon ground nutmeg
1/4 teaspoon ground allspice
1/4 teaspoon baking soda
1 can 100% pumpkin purée
2 eggs or 2 heaping tablespoons applesauce
1/4 teaspoon vanilla extract
1 cup chocolate chips
cooking spray

Preheat oven to 350 degrees. Combine all dry ingredients. Add pumpkin purée and eggs (or apple sauce). Add vanilla extract, to bring out pumpkin flavors. Stir in chocolate chips. Drop heaping tablespoons onto lightly sprayed cookie sheet. Bake for 15 to 20 minutes or until golden brown. Let cookies cool for 10 minutes on a wire rack.

Russian Cookies

Yield: 2 dozen cookies

2 egg yolks, beaten
1/4 cup butter or margarine
1 cup sugar
1/4 cup oil
1/4 cup sour cream
1 teaspoon vanilla
2 cups flour
salt
1 cup chopped pecans or walnuts
1 cup golden raisins
confectioners sugar

Blend eggs with butter and sugar. Add oil, sour cream and vanilla. Add flour, dash of salt, nuts and raisins. Blend well with hands. Divide dough into 3 parts (1 cup each). Shape each part into logs, 1 1/2 inch diameter. Place each log on a greased baking sheet. Bake at 350 degrees for 35 to 45 minutes. Remove from oven; sprinkle liberally with confectioners sugar while still warm. Cool and cut into 1 inch slices. Freezes well. Double recipe and keep in freezer.

Cinnamon Biscotti

Yield: 3 dozen biscotti

BISCOTTI DOUGH

parchment paper
1 cup unsalted butter, melted, set aside to cool
1 1/2 cups sugar (regular or baker's sugar*)
1/2 cup dark brown sugar, firmly packed
2 large eggs
1/4 cup buttermilk
1 teaspoon vanilla extract
1/2 teaspoon salt
2 1/2 teaspoons baking powder
1/4 teaspoon baking soda
3 cups all-purpose flour (more if necessary)

CINNAMON SUGAR MIXTURE

1/2 cup baker's sugar*
2 tablespoons cinnamon

Preheat oven to 350 degrees. Use 2 insulated cookie sheets; line each with parchment paper. With electric mixer, blend butter, sugars, eggs, buttermilk and vanilla. Fold in dry ingredients. If necessary, add more flour to make dough a consistency that can be shaped into a flat log. Using a spatula or wooden spoon, place dough onto cookie sheets. On each cookie sheet, shape into 2 flat loaves or rectangles, no larger than 4 inches across. Biscotti spread when baking. If dough is too sticky, wet your hands. Shaping dough will be much easier.

Bake until set, about 45 minutes. Allow to cool. Slice into 1/2 to 3/4 inch diagonal slices. Lay biscotti on its side. Return to oven at 325 degrees to lightly toast each side. When turning biscotti over, do so carefully, so as not to break them. This should take about 15 to 20 minutes. While biscotti is toasting, prepare cinnamon sugar mixture. Use a medium-size bowl to mix sugar and cinnamon together. Pour into a plastic bag. When biscotti have cooled slightly, gently coat each one.

Note: These may be kept at room temperature, tightly covered for several days, or frozen.

*Baker's sugar is an ultrafine sugar.

Mandelbrot

cooking spray
3 cups flour
2 1/4 teaspoons double-acting baking powder
3/4 teaspoon salt
1 cup sugar
3/4 cup vegetable oil
3 large eggs
3/4 to 1 teaspoon vanilla extract
1 1/2 teaspoons cinnamon
1 1/2 cups chocolate chips, optional
1 1/2 cups walnuts, optional

Preheat oven to 350 degrees. Spray 2 large baking sheets; sprinkle with flour. Sift together flour, baking powder and salt. Set aside. Beat together sugar and oil. Blend in eggs, one at a time. Add vanilla, cinnamon and flour mixture. Stir in chocolate chips and nuts. Using floured hands, form dough into 4 loaves, about 10x3x3/4 inches, smoothing tops. Dough will be very sticky, so frequent re-flouring of hands will be necessary. Bake until lightly browned, about 30 minutes. Remove from oven; cut with sharp knife into 1/2 inch slices. Place slices, cut side down, onto hot baking sheet; bake on both sides until lightly browned (5 to 10 minutes). Slices will harden as they cool. Store in airtight container. Makes about 50 slices.

Almond Tart

PASTRY
1 1/2 cups flour
1/2 cup sugar
2 teaspoons baking powder
1/4 pound (1 stick) unsalted butter, cut into pieces
1 teaspoon vanilla
2 eggs

Blend dry ingredients until crumbly. Add vanilla and eggs. If pastry is wet, add more flour. Refrigerate for 1 hour, wrapped in parchment paper.

FILLING
8 ounces sliced almonds
1 cup sugar
1/2 pound (2 sticks) unsalted butter
6 tablespoons milk
apricot jelly

Boil all ingredients for 10 minutes (excluding apricot jelly). Line large fluted pie dish with pastry. Prick with a fork and spread with apricot jelly. Bake tart shell for 10 minutes at 400 degrees. Remove from oven; carefully pour in filling. Put back in oven for 15 minutes, until tart is golden.

Nut-Free Mandelbrot

3 eggs
1 cup sugar
1 cup canola or safflower oil
1 teaspoon vanilla
3 cups flour
1 teaspoon baking powder
1/2 teaspoon salt
1 1/2 cups shredded, unsweetened baking coconut
1/2 cup golden raisins
1/2 cup semi-sweet chocolate chips
parchment paper

CINNAMON SUGAR, OPTIONAL

3 tablespoons sugar
1/2 teaspoon cinnamon

Beat eggs well in mixer. Add sugar, oil and vanilla; beat until well-blended. In another bowl, combine flour, baking powder and salt. Add dry ingredients to egg; mix well. Mix in coconut. Stir in raisins and chocolate chips. Mixture should be very thick. Refrigerate for 1 hour for easier handling. Preheat oven to 350 degrees. Line 2 baking sheets with parchment paper. Flour hands; form mixture into 4 long rolls, placing 2 rolls on each baking sheet. Bake for 30 minutes, rotating baking sheets halfway. Remove from oven when golden brown; let cool for 15 minutes. When cooled slightly, cut into 1-inch to 2-inch slices. Lay flat on baking sheet. Sprinkle with cinnamon sugar; bake on one side at 200 degrees for 30 minutes. Cool completely.

Apple Cake with Raisins

1 cup (2 sticks) butter or margarine
1 cup sugar
1 egg
1 cup flour
1 teaspoon baking soda
pinch of salt
1/2 cup raisins
1/2 cup nuts, optional
2 to 3 cups peeled, diced apples (preferably Granny Smith)
1 teaspoon vanilla
whipped cream, optional
ice cream, optional

Cream butter and sugar together. Add egg, flour, baking soda and salt. Fold in raisins, nuts and apples. Add vanilla. Bake at 350 degrees for 50 to 60 minutes in a lightly greased springform pan. Top with whipped cream or ice cream. Serve warm or at room temperature.

Marlene's Apple Cake

margarine or butter
flour
6 Granny Smith or similar apples, peeled, sliced, cut into half slices
1 1/3 cups plus 5 tablespoons sugar
5 teaspoons cinnamon
3 cups unbleached all-purpose flour
3 teaspoons baking powder
1 teaspoon salt
1 1/4 cups vegetable oil
4 eggs
1/2 cup orange juice
1 tablespoon vanilla extract

Preheat oven to 350 degrees. Grease a Bundt pan with margarine or butter. Dust with flour. Combine apples, 5 tablespoons sugar and cinnamon; set aside. Combine flour, baking powder and salt in medium-sized bowl. Add remaining 1 1/3 cups sugar. Add oil, eggs, orange juice and vanilla. Mix well. Pour 1/3 of batter into Bundt pan. Add 1/2 of apple slices. Add another 1/3 of batter and add rest of apple slices. Cover with remaining batter. Bake approximately 1 hour, until top is golden brown, and toothpick inserted into thickest part of the cake comes out dry.

Note: This cake is extremely versatile. Other fruits can be substituted for the apples, such as fresh blueberries when in season. For a more decadent version, try using chocolate chips and nuts instead of the fruit!

Banana Cake

CAKE BATTER

- 1 1/2 cups sugar
- 4 eggs
- 1 cup margarine
- 3 cups flour
- 4 bananas (very ripe and soft)
- 1 cup orange juice
- 1 teaspoon salt
- 1 teaspoon vanilla
- 2 teaspoons baking soda

Cream sugar, eggs and margarine. Add rest of ingredients. Blend well. Pour into greased 9x13 pan.

CINNAMON-SUGAR NUT TOPPING

- 1 teaspoon cinnamon
- 1/2 cup sugar
- 1 cup chopped walnuts

Mix cinnamon, sugar and nuts. Top cake and bake at 350 degrees for 50 to 60 minutes.

Chocolate Bundt Recipe

- 1 18.25 ounce package devil's food cake mix
- 1 5 ounce package chocolate pudding mix
- 1/4 cup warm water
- 1/2 cup oil
- 8 ounces sour cream
- 4 eggs
- cooking spray
- 8 ounces chocolate chips
- 1 8 ounce carton non-dairy whipped topping

Mix first 6 ingredients together for 2 minutes in a bowl. Spray Bundt pan with nonstick spray and pour batter into pan. Add chocolate chips and mix well. Place in preheated 350 degree oven for 50 minutes. Test with toothpick to make sure cake is done. Cool. Top with non-dairy whipped topping.

Best Pareve Chocolate Cake

Yield: Two 8-inch layers

parchment paper
1 1/2 cups (3 sticks) pareve margarine, room temperature, plus more for pan
1 cup cocoa powder, plus more for dusting
3/4 cup strong coffee, boiling
1 cup almond milk, room temperature
2 3/4 cups cake flour (not self-rising)
1 teaspoon baking soda
1/2 teaspoon salt
2 1/2 cups sugar
1 tablespoon vanilla extract
4 large eggs, room temperature

Place rack in middle of oven. Preheat oven to 350 degrees. Grease two 8x2 round cake pans and line with parchment paper. Grease parchment paper and dust with cocoa powder. Tap out excess. Sift cocoa; whisk in coffee and almond milk. Let cool. Sift together cake flour, baking soda and salt. Set aside.

Beat margarine in a large bowl, until light and fluffy, about 2 minutes (You can use your stand mixer with paddle attachment.) Gradually add sugar and vanilla. Add eggs one at a time, stirring well after each addition. Pour in cooled cocoa mixture. Mix until fully incorporated.

Add sifted dry ingredients to chocolate mixture, stirring until just combined. Pour batter into prepared pans (about 4 cups in each pan). Bake for 20 minutes, rotate pans and bake for an additional 15 minutes, until a cake tester comes out clean, when inserted into center.

Remove cakes from oven and allow to cool in pans for 15 minutes on a cooling rack. Carefully run a small offset spatula around edge of cakes to loosen them from pan. Remove cakes from pans and invert onto a wire rack. Let cool completely (about 1 hour).

FROSTING

3 1/2 cups confectioners sugar
1 cup cocoa powder
12 tablespoons (1 1/2 sticks) pareve margarine, room temperature
1/2 cup almond milk, room temperature
2 teaspoons vanilla extract

In a mixing bowl, sift together confectioners sugar and cocoa powder. Add margarine, almond milk and vanilla, stir (or mix in stand-mixer fitted with paddle attachment) until smooth and free of lumps. Refrigerate until firm. Make sure frosting is chilled when frosting cake or texture will be too soft to work with.

To assemble: using a serrated knife, level top surface of each cake layer. The top surface tends to become a little crusty. To frost cake, put cut-side down and generously spread with frosting. Top with remaining layer, bottom side up. Put a thin coat of frosting over entire cake and chill until frosting is firm. Remove cake from refrigerator and finish frosting. Chill cake until ready to serve.

Cake with Fruit Filling

Cake needs to be made in a pan with a hole in it. A Bundt pan is too deep. Grease pan well and, if desired, sprinkle with brown sugar and a bit of cinnamon.

3 eggs
1 teaspoon vanilla
3/4 cup oil
2/3 cup sugar
1 1/2 cups flour
1 teaspoon baking powder
1 can cherry, blueberry or apple pie filling
1/2 cup brown sugar
1 teaspoon cinnamon

This can be made in a mixer or food processor, but can also be beaten together with a fork in a bowl!

Beat eggs and vanilla together. Add oil, sugar, flour and baking powder, beating after each addition. Pour 1/2 of batter into a well-greased springform pan. Spread pie filling over dough. Cover with rest of dough, spreading with your fingers. Dough will spread while baking. Mix brown sugar and cinnamon; sprinkle over cake. Bake at 350 degrees for about 45 minutes, or until a tester comes out clean. Do not double this recipe. Can be frozen.

Cool well. Run a spatula around inside of pan. Remove sides of springform pan when cool. Run spatula around center of pan. Flip cake over onto a plate and then flip over again so top-side is up.

Pumpkin Pie Cake

4 eggs, beaten
1 29 ounce can pumpkin
1 12 ounce can evaporated milk
1 1/2 cups sugar
2 teaspoons cinnamon
1 teaspoon ginger
1 1/2 teaspoons nutmeg
1 box yellow cake mix (not pudding style)
1 cup butter, melted
1 cup chopped nuts

Beat eggs in large bowl. Add pumpkin, evaporated milk, sugar, cinnamon, ginger and nutmeg. Beat ingredients together. Pour into greased 9x13 cake pan. Sprinkle dry cake mix over mixture. Pour melted butter over cake mix. Sprinkle chopped nuts over top. Bake at 350 degrees for 1 hour.

Chocolate Chip Cake

1/4 pound butter or margarine
1 1/2 cups sugar, divided
2 eggs
1 cup sour cream
1 teaspoon vanilla
2 cups flour
1 1/2 teaspoons baking powder
1 teaspoon baking soda
1 teaspoon cinnamon
1 cup chocolate chips

Cream butter, 1 cup sugar and eggs in mixer. Add sour cream and vanilla. Add flour, baking powder and baking soda to butter mixture; beat. Pour half of batter into greased angel food pan. In separate bowl, mix 1/2 cup sugar, cinnamon and chocolate chips. Spoon half over cake batter. Add remainder of cake batter and top with remainder of chocolate chip mixture. Bake for 45 minutes at 350 degrees. Cool and remove from pan.

Chocolate Nut Coffee Cake

1/2 cup butter or margarine
1 1/2 cups sugar, divided
2 eggs or egg substitute equivalent
1 cup sour cream
1 teaspoon vanilla
1 cup white flour
1 cup whole-wheat flour
1 1/2 teaspoons baking powder
1 teaspoon baking soda
1 teaspoon cinnamon
1 cup chocolate chips (6 ounces)
1/2 cup chopped pecans or walnuts

In a mixer bowl, beat together butter and 1 cup of sugar until creamy. Add eggs, one at a time, and beat until fluffy. Mix in sour cream and vanilla. Combine flours, baking powder and baking soda. Stir into creamed mixture. Mix together remaining 1/2 cup sugar, cinnamon, chocolate chips and nuts. Lightly mix half of sugar-cinnamon mixture with batter and spread into greased 9x13 pan. Sprinkle remaining half over top; press sugar-cinnamon mixture into batter with back of spoon. Bake in a 350 degree oven for 35 minutes or until a wooden pick inserted comes out clean.

Fantastic Carrot Cake

CAKE

- 2 cups flour
- 2 teaspoons baking soda
- 3 large eggs
- 2 cups sugar
- 1 teaspoon cinnamon
- 1 teaspoon salt
- 1 1/4 cups oil
- 2 cups shredded carrots
- 3 1/2 ounces sweetened, shredded coconut
- 1 cup canned crushed pineapple, fruit and juice
- 1 cup chopped nuts, optional

Mix all ingredients together and bake in 9x13 pan at 350 degrees for 50 minutes. Cool on cake rack completely before frosting.

FROSTING

- 4 tablespoons butter
- 12 ounces cream cheese
- 4 cups confectioners sugar, sifted
- 1/2 teaspoon salt
- 4 teaspoons vanilla

Blend all ingredients together and frost cake.

Note: This cake can make two 8 or 9 inch round cakes as well. Adjust baking time for smaller cakes.

1-Bowl-Method Passover Sponge Cake

- wax paper
- 10 eggs
- 2 cups sugar
- 1/4 teaspoon salt
- 1 cup matzah cake meal
- 1/3 cup orange juice with 1 teaspoon lemon juice
- 1/3 cup potato starch

Use a 10 inch tube pan – trace bottom and hole of pan on wax paper. Cut out circle and hole and place wax paper in bottom of tube pan. Wrap wax paper around funnel on inside of pan and stuff some wax paper inside hole. Beat eggs with mixer for at least 20 minutes or until bowl is almost full. Add sugar and salt; keep beating. Add cake meal; beat. Add juice; beat. Add potato starch and beat for 1 minute or until mixed. Pour into ungreased pan (with wax paper) and bake in a preheated oven for 1 hour at 350 degrees. Turn upside down on funnel or (wine) bottle and allow cake to cool in pan. Use a thin pliable knife to loosen sides.

New York Cheesecake

Yield: Serves 8

COOKIE CRUST

1/2 cup butter, softened*
1/2 cup granulated sugar
1/2 teaspoon vanilla
dash of salt
1 egg
1 1/2 cups flour
nonstick spray

Cream together butter, sugar, vanilla and salt. Add egg. Mix well. Add flour. Stir well to combine. Preheat oven to 375 degrees. Lightly spray a 9-inch springform pan bottom with nonstick spray. Press half of dough onto bottom of pan. Bake for 5 to 7 minutes or until edge of dough begins to turn light brown. Cool. When pan has cooled, lightly spray sides of pan with nonstick spray. Take remaining dough and press it around inside edge of pan. (Don't go all the way to top; leave about 1/2-inch margin from top of pan.)

FILLING

40 ounces cream cheese, softened*
1 1/3 cups sugar
2 teaspoons vanilla extract
2 teaspoons lemon juice
1/3 cup sour cream
2 tablespoons flour
3 eggs

Turn oven temperature up to 500 degrees. Combine cream cheese, sugar, vanilla and lemon juice with electric mixer, in a large bowl, until smooth. Mix in sour cream and flour. Add eggs. Mix on low-speed until combined. Pour cream cheese filling into pan. Bake for 10 minutes. Reduce heat to 350 degrees. Bake for 30 to 35 minutes, until center is firm. Cover. Cool in refrigerator for several hours or overnight before serving.

*Leave butter and cream cheese out of refrigerator for 30 to 60 minutes to soften.

Pumpkin Spice Cake

1 2/3 cups sifted flour
1 teaspoon baking soda
1 teaspoon salt
1/2 teaspoon baking powder
1 teaspoon cinnamon
1 teaspoon nutmeg
1/4 teaspoon ginger
1/4 teaspoon ground cloves
1 cup light brown sugar, packed
1/3 cup margarine
1 cup canned pumpkin
1/2 cup water
1 egg
1/2 cup chopped walnuts
1/2 cup raisins
lemon sauce, optional
whipped cream, optional

Sift together flour, baking soda, salt, baking powder, cinnamon, nutmeg, ginger and cloves into a large bowl of an electric mixer. Add sugar, margarine, pumpkin and water. Beat at medium speed for 2 minutes. Add egg and beat 2 minutes longer. Add nuts and raisins; mix. Turn into a greased and lightly floured 10-inch tube pan or Bundt pan. Bake at 350 degrees for 45 to 50 minutes or until cake pulls away from sides of pan and cake tester inserted near center comes out clean. Turn out of pan to cool and serve plain or with lemon sauce or whipped cream. It is better to bake one or two days before serving. The longer it sits, the moister it is.

Note: Double recipe if using large Bundt pan.

Rum Cake

CAKE

unsalted margarine
1 cup finely chopped walnuts or pecans
1 package yellow cake mix
1 3.4 ounce package instant vanilla pudding mix
4 eggs
1/2 cup cold water
1/2 cup oil
1/2 cup dark rum

GLAZE

1 stick unsalted margarine (1/4 pound)
1/4 cup water
1 cup granulated sugar
1/2 cup dark rum

Heat oven to 325 degrees. Grease 10-inch tube or Bundt pan with unsalted margarine, sprinkle nuts over bottom of pan. Combine in mixer: cake mix, pudding mix, eggs, water, oil and rum. Pour batter over nuts; bake one hour. Cool for 15 minutes. Meanwhile, prepare glaze. Using pan with thick bottom, melt margarine slowly in water and sugar. Bring to a boil, stirring continuously for 5 minutes, while mixture boils. Remove from heat and stir in rum. Cool slightly. Put cake onto platter. Prick top and sides evenly with toothpick. Drizzle and smooth glaze evenly over top and sides. Allow cake to absorb glaze and repeat until glaze is used up. Refrigerate covered. Will stay moist and delicious for days. Can be frozen.

Strawberry Sandwich Cookie Sponge Cake Dessert

1 sponge cake or angel food cake
12 to 24 chocolate sandwich cookies (or more, if desired)
2 boxes fresh strawberries, hulled
6 tablespoons sugar (or more, to taste)
1 lemon, squeezed
whipped cream

Pinch pieces of sponge cake into 8×8 inch dish. Cover with ground-up chocolate sandwich cookies, to desired layer of thickness. In a skillet, crush strawberries. Sauté with sugar and a dash of lemon juice until saucy. Pour the strawberry purée over cookies and place in refrigerator for 2 hours. When strawberry mixture has cooled, top with lots of whipped cream.

Strawberry Sorbet

1 quart strawberries, hulled
1 1/2 cups sugar
2 tablespoons lemon juice
3 egg whites, beaten stiff

Blend together, in a blender or food processor, strawberries, sugar and lemon juice. Fold in egg whites. Put in freezer until almost frozen. Remove from freezer and blend again in small batches. Freeze. Can be kept in freezer for several months.

Luscious Chocolate Mousse

6 ounces semi-sweet chocolate
6 egg yolks
1/3 cup sugar
rind of 1 orange, finely grated
6 egg whites
whipped cream, for decorating

Melt chocolate in top of double boiler and add slightly beaten egg yolks. Cook, stirring with a wooden spoon, for a few minutes. Do not let water in bottom of double boiler reach a boil. Remove from stove; mix in sugar and orange rind. Beat egg whites until stiff and fold in with metal spoon. Put into a bowl, chill and decorate with whipped cream.

Sandra's Ice Cream Mold

28 macaroons, divided
1 quart vanilla ice cream, slightly softened
4 tablespoons or more chocolate syrup, divided
1 quart chocolate ice cream, slightly softened
1/2 pound English Toffee

Oil an 8-inch springform pan. Crush 14 macaroons and spread on bottom of pan. Spread vanilla ice cream on top of crushed macaroons. Dribble 2 tablespoons chocolate syrup over ice cream. Crush remaining macaroons and spread on top of ice cream layer. Spread chocolate ice cream on top of second layer of macaroons. Dribble remaining chocolate syrup over ice cream. Crush English Toffee and spread on top. Place mold in freezer for 4 to 5 hours.

Variation: To use a larger springform pan, buy 1/2 gallon each flavor ice cream and fill to top of pan. The larger size will serve 12 to 16. Substitute any flavor ice cream.

Gelatin Fluff

1 6 ounce package lemon gelatin (or any flavor)
2 cups hot water
2 cups regular or diet lemon-lime soda
juice of 1 lemon
1 8 ounce carton non-dairy whipped topping

Dissolve gelatin in hot water. Add soda and lemon juice. Refrigerate until partially set (about 2 hours), then fold in non-dairy whipped topping. Refrigerate until cooled completely.

Note: This comes out light and fluffy and is so refreshing.

Apple Bread Pudding

Yield: Serves 10

1/2 pound day-old French bread, torn into pieces
1 cup coarsely chopped apples
1 cup chopped nuts
2 cups milk
2 cups half-and-half
3 eggs, beaten
1 cup brown sugar, packed
1/2 cup sugar
1/4 cup dark rum
3/4 tablespoon vanilla

Combine bread, apples and nuts in large bowl, toss gently. Combine milk and half-and-half, pour over bread mixture. Cover and chill one hour. Combine eggs, sugars, rum and vanilla, stir well. Add egg mixture to chilled bread mixture, stir gently to combine. Pour into greased 9x13x2 pan.
Bake, uncovered, at 325 degrees for 1 hour or until set and lightly browned.

Hawaiian Bread Pudding

3 eggs
1 1/2 cups sugar, divided
1 quart milk
1 teaspoon cinnamon
12 ounces white bread, cut into cubes (about 1/2 loaf)
4 ounces melted butter
1/4 to 1/2 cup dark raisins
1/2 teaspoon vanilla
1/2 cup apricot-pineapple jam

Mix eggs with half of sugar. Add milk to egg-sugar mix. Mix cinnamon with rest of sugar. Add cinnamon-sugar mixture to milk mixture. Add cubes of bread. Add melted butter, raisins, vanilla and jam. Mix and let sit for 1 hour in refrigerator. Using an 8x11 glass ovenproof baking dish, bake at 400 degrees. Use a water bath for 30 to 45 minutes while pudding cooks.

Land of Nod Cinnamon Buns

20 frozen dough rolls
1 cup brown sugar
1/4 cup vanilla instant pudding
1 to 2 tablespoons cinnamon
3/4 cup raisins, optional
1/4 to 1/2 cup melted butter

The night before, grease a 10-inch Bundt pan and add frozen rolls. Sprinkle with brown sugar, pudding powder, cinnamon and raisins. Pour melted butter over all. Cover with a clean, damp cloth (leave out at room temperature). In the morning, preheat oven to 350 degrees and bake for 25 minutes. Let sit for 5 minutes and then turn out on a serving plate.

Travadicos

Yield: 30 Travadicos

DOUGH

1 cup vegetable oil
1/2 cup semi-sweet white wine
1/4 cup sugar
1/8 teaspoon salt
1/4 teaspoon cinnamon
1/4 teaspoon baking soda
3 1/2 cups all-purpose flour

FILLING

2 cups coarsely chopped walnuts
1/4 cup orange marmalade
1/8 teaspoon ground cinnamon

SYRUP

1 cup honey
1/2 cup water
1/2 cup sugar

Combine dough ingredients and mix well. Allow to rest while preparing filling. To make filling, mix walnuts, marmalade and cinnamon. Set aside. Divide dough into walnut-sized balls. With rolling pin, roll each ball into a 3-inch circle. Place a scant teaspoon of filling in center of each circle. Fold circle in half to enclose filling. Pinch edges of dough together with fingers. Place on cookie sheet. Bake in preheated 350 degree oven for 20 minutes, or until lightly browned. While Travadicos are baking, prepare syrup. Boil honey, water and sugar together until sticky enough to coat back of spoon, about 10 minutes. Cool slightly. Cool Travadicos on cookie sheets. Dip in warm syrup. Remove and allow syrup to permeate pastries one to two hours before serving.

Nut Filled Filo Rolls (Travados)

Yield: 40 Travados

2 cups chopped or ground walnuts
1 cup almonds, blanched and finely chopped
2 teaspoons sugar
1/4 teaspoon cinnamon
1/4 teaspoon nutmeg, optional
1 pound filo dough
melted butter

Mix nuts, sugar and spices. Brush half of each sheet of filo dough with melted butter and fold over the other half, brushing with butter, so you have a double piece of filo 12x7 1/2 inches. Sprinkle with 1 tablespoon mixture beginning at short end. Roll filo as you would a jelly-roll. Cut in half, making two rolls approximately 3 1/2 inches in length. Repeat with each sheet with folded sides down. Brush with melted butter and bake in moderate oven for 15 to 20 minutes until golden brown. While hot, dip into warm syrup.

SYRUP

1 cup sugar
1/4 cup honey
1 teaspoon lemon juice
2/3 cup water
small stick cinnamon

Mix syrup ingredients together in a pan and dissolve over low flame. Cool syrup before dipping nut rolls.

Apple Dulce

1 1/2 cups water
2 cups sugar
juice of 1/2 lemon
5 apples, peeled and sliced
5 to 6 whole cloves

Boil water and sugar until slightly thick. Add lemon juice. Dip apples into syrup until partially cooked, yet still firm. Remove from heat. Add cloves and let cool. Refrigerate.

Stacy's Fantastic Chocolate Hard Toffee

1 10 ounce bar dark chocolate
2 cups (4 sticks) butter (salted or unsalted)
2 cups sugar
3 tablespoons water
1 1/2 cups chopped nuts, if desired (almonds, cashews, pecans, etc.)

Break chocolate into small pieces and set aside. Bring butter to bubble. Add sugar, stir constantly until mixed. Add water. Keep at a high temperature and keep stirring. Mixture will continue to bubble and turn darker. Stir until mixture is a dark caramel color. Add nuts, if desired. Stir a bit more. Pour onto greased cookie sheet. Let toffee sit for about 4 to 5 minutes. It needs to cool enough so that chocolate you set on top doesn't sink in, but remains hot enough to melt chocolate. Set chocolate pieces on top. Let melt and then spread evenly with spatula. When toffee is completely cooled, break into pieces. Stays best uncovered or freeze until ready to serve.

Hot Fruit Compote

1 large can sliced peaches
1 large can sliced pears
1 large can apricots
2 cans pineapple chunks
2 large firm bananas, sliced on angle
1 can cherry pie filling
1/2 cup dry white wine

TOPPING
2 tablespoons flour
2 tablespoons melted butter
1/2 cup ground walnuts
1/4 cup brown sugar
1 tablespoon cinnamon

Drain canned fruit on paper towels, (not including bananas or cherry pie filling) for several days. Place an assortment of fruit plus bananas into low baking dish. Spread with layer of cherry pie filling. Repeat ending with cherry pie filling. Pour wine over layers of fruit. Combine all ingredients for topping and spread over fruit. Bake at 350 degrees for 45 minutes.

Summer Fruit Trifle

Yield: Serves 12-18

12 ounces cream cheese, room temperature
1/2 cup plus 2 tablespoons sugar, divided
2 cups whipping cream, chilled
2 teaspoons vanilla extract
4 nectarines, halved, pitted, thinly sliced
2 1/2 pint containers raspberries
1 pint container blueberries
1 teaspoon ground cinnamon
6 tablespoons apricot jam
3 tablespoons dark rum
1 1/2 12 ounce purchased pound cakes, cut into 1/2-inch-thick slices

Beat cream cheese and 1/2 cup sugar in large bowl until fluffy. Gradually beat in cream. Add vanilla and beat until medium-stiff peaks form. Set cheese mixture aside. Combine all fruits, remaining 2 tablespoons sugar and cinnamon in another large bowl. Mix jam and rum in small bowl to blend. Arrange enough cake slices in bottom of 3-quart trifle dish to cover. Brush with 3 tablespoons jam mixture. Top with 2 cups fruit mixture. Top with half of cream cheese mixture. Top with another layer of cake slices. Brush with 3 tablespoons jam mixture. Top with 2 cups fruit mixture, then remaining cream cheese mixture. Cover with another layer of cake. Brush with remaining jam mixture. Top with remaining fruit mixture. Cover and refrigerate at least 3 hours and up to 8 hours.

Mandelbrot

Yield: 42 Mandelbrot pieces

3 eggs
1 cup sugar
1 cup oil (not safflower)
1 teaspoon vanilla
2 3/4 cups flour
1/4 teaspoon salt
1 cup chopped walnuts
1 cup chocolate chips
1/2 cup sugar
1 tablespoon cinnamon

Stir together eggs, sugar, oil and vanilla in a bowl. Add flour and salt to mixture. Add nuts and chips to mixture. Divide dough into 3 oval flats and place on cookie sheet. Bake at 375 degrees for 30 minutes. Remove from oven and cut into strips on cookie sheet. Mix sugar and cinnamon together; sprinkle over cookies. Put back in oven for 10 minutes. Cool. Can be frozen.

Apple Cake

1 cup sugar
2 cups peeled, sliced apples (3 large apples)
1/4 cup oil
1 egg, beaten
1 teaspoon vanilla
1 cup flour
1 teaspoon cinnamon
1 teaspoon baking soda
1/4 teaspoon salt
1/2 cup chopped walnuts
whipped cream, optional
ice cream, optional

Preheat oven to 350 degrees. Grease 8-inch square baking pan. In a bowl, sprinkle sugar over sliced apples; let stand for 20 minutes. Add oil, egg and vanilla to apple/sugar mixture. Combine flour with cinnamon, baking soda and salt. Stir flour mixture into apples. Add nuts. Bake for 50 minutes. If doubling recipe, bake in 9x12 pan.

Note: This cake is best when eaten same day. Keep leftovers refrigerated. Serve warm with whipped cream or ice cream.

Passover Farfel Lace Cookies

Yield: 15-18 cookies

1 cup farfel
3/4 to 1 cup sugar
1 tablespoon Passover cake meal
1/2 cup ground almonds or toasted slivered almonds
dash of salt
1 egg
1/2 teaspoon vanilla
1/4 cup melted butter

Mix farfel, sugar, cake meal, almonds and salt. In separate bowl, mix egg and vanilla. Add to dry ingredients. Add melted butter. Stir constantly. Line cookie sheets with aluminum foil. Place 1 tablespoon of batter 2 inches apart (they spread). Bake at 325 degrees for 8 to 10 minutes or until golden brown. Lift foil from cookie sheet. When cool, remove cookies.

Chocolate Passover Cookies

Yield: 14 cookies

4 tablespoons unsalted butter or non-dairy margarine, room temperature
3/4 cup packed light-brown sugar
2 large egg yolks
1 teaspoon vanilla extract
9 ounces bittersweet chocolate, melted
1/2 cup matzo meal
1/4 teaspoon coarse salt
4 large egg whites
8 ounces semi-sweet chocolate chips

Preheat oven to 350 degrees. Beat butter or margarine and sugar with mixer on medium-high speed until fluffy. Beat in egg yolks and vanilla. Add chocolate, matzo meal and salt. Beat until mixture just comes together (it should be thick). In clean bowl, with whisk attachment, beat egg whites until stiff peaks form. Gently fold into chocolate mixture. Add chocolate chips and stir. Let stand 15 minutes. Scoop 2-inch balls onto parchment-lined baking sheet. Bake until set, 10 to 12 minutes. Let cool on sheet on wire rack for 2 minutes. Transfer cookies to rack and let cool completely.

I Can't Believe It's Not Ice Cream

2 egg whites
3/4 cup sugar
1 10 ounce package frozen strawberries, mostly thawed or fresh sugared strawberries
1 tablespoon lemon juice
dash of salt
sweet wine (to taste – a few tablespoons)
shaved chocolate or chopped nuts for garnish

In a 5-quart or larger bowl of electric mixer, beat egg whites and sugar until stiff. Toss in strawberries. Add lemon juice, salt and wine. Start on low speed and increase for 15 minutes (in last 2 to 3 minutes it gets really big). Spoon into serving bowl and freeze.

Defrost for about 1 hour at room temperature for easier serving. Top with chocolate or nuts to garnish.

Note: Can be put on angel food cake and topped with strawberry slices and non-dairy whipped topping.

Passover Apple Cobbler

Prep: 1 hour, 15 minutes

8 apples, peeled, cored, thickly sliced
3/4 cup sugar
1 tablespoon lemon juice
1 teaspoon vanilla
cinnamon, to taste
1/4 teaspoon salt
2 tablespoons oil
1 box Passover coffee cake mix

Preheat oven to 375 degrees. Combine all ingredients, except cake mix. Arrange in a 2-quart baking dish. Prepare cake mix according to package directions. Spoon cake mixture on top of apple mixture. Prepare crumb topping from package according to directions and sprinkle on top of batter. Bake for 45 minutes to 1 hour.

Passover Apple Nut Cake

CAKE

2 3/4 cups sugar, divided
2 teaspoons cinnamon
juice of 1 lemon
6 eggs
1 cup oil
2 cups matzo cake meal
2 teaspoons potato starch
5 apples, peeled, cored and sliced

TOPPING

1/4 cup sugar
2 teaspoons cinnamon
1/4 cup chopped walnuts

Combine 3/4 cup sugar, cinnamon and lemon juice. Set aside. Beat eggs with remaining 2 cups sugar until mixture is light and fluffy. Beat in oil. Sift together cake meal and potato starch. Add to egg mixture, blending well. Pour half of batter into 9x13 greased pan. Spread apples over batter. Top with remaining batter.

Make topping by combining sugar, cinnamon and walnuts. Sprinkle over cake. Bake in preheated 350 degree oven for 1 hour and 15 minutes. (Check after 1 hour to see if you need additional time.)

Passover Chocolate Chip Cookies

Yield: 4-5 dozen
Prep: 15 minutes

1 1/2 cups firmly packed brown sugar
1/2 cup sugar
2 tablespoons Passover vanilla sugar or 1 teaspoon vanilla
1 cup unsalted butter or margarine
2 eggs
1/4 teaspoon salt, optional
1/2 cup matzo meal
1/2 cup matzo cake meal
1 cup potato starch
2 cups chocolate chips

Cream sugars together with vanilla sugar or vanilla and butter or margarine. Blend in eggs. Stir in salt, matzo meal, cake meal, potato starch and chocolate chips. Chill dough for an hour or overnight (it also freezes well). Preheat oven to 350 degrees. Line a couple of baking sheets with parchment paper. Scoop teaspoons of dough onto baking sheets, leaving room for them to spread. Bake in preheated oven for about 12 minutes. Let cookies sit on baking sheets for 10 to 15 minutes, until just cool. Using metal spatula, transfer to cooling racks to finish cooling completely.

Passover Matzah Brittle

Yield: Serves 15
Prep: 15 minutes

7 matzahs
1 1/2 cups margarine
1 1/2 cups brown sugar
1 cup chocolate chips
cashews or almonds, as desired
marshmallows, as desired

Line the bottom of a 4-sided cookie sheet with matzah. Combine margarine and brown sugar. Bring to a boil. Pour the mixture over the matzah. Bake for 8 to 10 minutes, until golden brown. While hot, add chocolate chips; spread evenly. Add nuts and/or marshmallows as desired. Refrigerate until hard. Break into pieces. Keep refrigerated.

Note: This is a great snack during Passover.

Passover Lemon Squares

CRUST

2 cans macaroons
1 egg, beaten

In food processor, chop macaroons. Then mold into 10x10 glass ovenproof baking dish. Brush with egg and bake at 350 degrees for 8 to 10 minutes.

FILLING

4 large egg yolks
3 large eggs
1/2 cup granulated sugar
3/4 cup fresh lemon juice
2 tablespoons potato starch
1 stick chilled butter, cut into small pieces

In double boiler, whisk together egg yolks, eggs, sugar, lemon juice and potato starch. Place over simmering water. Cook over medium heat, stirring constantly, until thick enough to coat back of a spoon. Do not let mixture boil. Remove mixture from over water. Stir in butter. Pour onto crust.

MERINGUE

4 large egg whites
1/4 teaspoon potato starch
1/4 teaspoon cream of tartar
1/4 cup superfine sugar
1 teaspoon vanilla extract

Beat egg whites at medium speed until foamy. Beat in potato starch and cream of tartar until soft peaks form. Gradually beat in sugar and vanilla at high speed until stiff, but not dry, peaks form. Place meringue on top of filling. Bake at 350 degrees for 12 to 15 minutes or until golden brown. Cool completely and cut into squares.

Passover Apple Cake

3 eggs
3/4 cup sugar
1/3 cup oil
3/4 cup Passover cake meal
4 to 5 medium apples, peeled, cored and sliced
2 teaspoons cinnamon
1/2 cup sugar

Preheat oven to 350 degrees. Beat eggs with sugar and oil until mixture is light colored. Add cake meal and mix well. Pour half of batter mixture into greased 8-inch or 9-inch pan. Cover with half of apples. Pour rest of batter over apples. Cover with rest of apples, overlapping slices. Sprinkle with cinnamon and sugar over final layer of apples. Bake for 1 1/2 hours.

Brunch

Brunch

Pumpkin Bread

3 1/2 cups flour
2 cups sugar
1/2 teaspoon nutmeg
2 teaspoons cinnamon
1 teaspoon salt
2 teaspoons baking soda
1 cup vegetable oil
2/3 cup orange juice
4 eggs
1 1 pound can pumpkin puree
1 1/2 teaspoons vanilla
1 cup raisins, chopped nuts or chocolate chips

Combine flour, sugar, nutmeg, cinnamon, salt and baking soda in a large bowl. Add oil, orange juice and eggs. Beat well with electric mixer or by hand. Add pumpkin, while continuing to mix. Stir in raisins, nuts or chocolate chips. Pour batter into 2 greased 9x5 baking pans. Bake in preheated 350 degree oven for 1 hour or until bread tests done with a toothpick.

Cindy's Zucchini Bread

Yield: 2 loaves

3 eggs
1 cup oil
2 cups sugar
2 cups grated unpeeled zucchini
1 cup chopped nuts

SIFT

2 cups white flour
1 cup whole-wheat flour
1 teaspoon salt
1 teaspoon baking soda
3 teaspoons cinnamon
1/4 teaspoon baking powder

Beat eggs. Add next 4 ingredients. Add sifted ingredients to wet mixture. Pour batter into 2 greased standard loaf pans or 4 small loaf pans. Bake at 325 degrees for 1 hour.

Incredible Pumpkin Bread

2 large eggs
1 cup sugar
1 cup canned pumpkin
1/2 cup vegetable or canola oil
1/2 cup orange juice
2 cups all-purpose flour
1 teaspoon baking soda
1/2 teaspoon baking powder
1/2 teaspoon ground cinnamon
1/2 teaspoon ground cloves
1/2 teaspoon ground nutmeg
1/2 teaspoon ground ginger
1/2 cup chopped walnuts
1/2 cup chopped dates
1/3 cup chopped dried apricots

In large bowl, beat eggs, sugar, pumpkin, oil and orange juice. Stir flour with baking soda, baking powder, cinnamon, cloves, nutmeg and ginger. Add dry ingredients to egg mixture; beat to blend. Stir into greased 9x5 loaf pan or fill smaller loaf pans halfway. Bake at 350 degrees until toothpick comes clean, about 1 hour. Cool 15 minutes, run knife around pan edge, invert onto plate. Makes 1 loaf, about 2 1/2 pounds.

Banana Bread

1/2 cup butter or margarine
1 cup sugar
2 eggs
3 cups sifted flour
1 teaspoon baking soda
1/2 teaspoon salt
3 large bananas (mashed)
4 tablespoons melted unsalted butter, divided
1 cup chopped walnuts, divided
1 teaspoon each, cinnamon and sugar

Cream butter and sugar; beat in eggs one at a time. Sift dry ingredients and mix together. Beat in mashed bananas. Add 1/2 cup walnuts. Pour into greased and floured 9x5x3 pan. Bake at 350 degrees for 50 to 60 minutes. While cake is warm, pour 1 tablespoon melted butter over top. Mix remainder of melted butter and rest of walnuts. Sprinkle over hot cake. Sprinkle with cinnamon and sugar.

Betty's Date Nut Loaf

2 tablespoons margarine
1/2 teaspoon vanilla
1 cup hot water
1 egg
1 1/4 cups all-purpose flour
1 teaspoon baking powder
1 teaspoon baking soda
1/2 cup sugar
1/4 teaspoon salt
1/2 teaspoon cinnamon
1 dash nutmeg, optional
1 dash cardamom, optional
1 8 ounce package chopped pitted dates
1/2 cup golden raisins
1/2 cup chopped walnuts

In small bowl, stir together margarine, vanilla and hot water; when margarine is melted and has cooled, stir in egg. In larger bowl, stir together flour, baking powder, baking soda, sugar, salt, cinnamon, nutmeg, cardamom, dates, raisins and walnuts. Pour margarine mixture into dry ingredients; stir until well blended. Pour batter into a greased 4 1/2x8 1/2 loaf pan. Bake at 325 degrees for 50 minutes or when toothpick comes out clean. Serve warm with cream cheese.

Blender French Toast

Yield: Serves 5

1 ripe banana
1 medium peach (or any soft seasonal fruit)
1/4 cup milk
3 eggs
2 teaspoons maple syrup
1/2 teaspoon vanilla
pinch of salt
10 slices challah bread
melted margarine or butter

Peel and slice bananas and peach into blender container. Add milk, eggs, maple syrup, vanilla and salt. Blend well. Turn into shallow pan. Soak bread in mixture 3 to 4 minutes; fry in melted margarine/butter until browned on 1 side, then other side.

Italian Cracked Wheat Bread

1/4 cup cracked bulgur wheat
3/4 cup boiling water

Pour water over bulgur wheat. Let sit at least 30 minutes.

1 cup warm water (105-115 degrees)
1 teaspoon yeast
2 teaspoons honey
1 cup cool water
1 cup whole-wheat flour
1 1/2 cups bread flour
1 teaspoon salt
2 cups all-purpose flour, approximately
1 egg and 1 teaspoon water, mix thoroughly in separate bowl

In mixing bowl or electric stand mixer, combine warm water, yeast and honey. Let sit until bubbly (approximately 10 minutes). Add cool water, whole-wheat flour and bread flour. Mix until smooth. Cover loosely with plastic wrap and let sit for 4 to 8 hours. May have to be deflated. Add cracked wheat, salt and enough all-purpose flour to make a sticky dough that still barely holds its shape. Turn onto floured surface and knead, adding enough all-purpose flour to keep from sticking, until elastic. Cover and let rest for 30 minutes. Form into desired shapes and place on greased baking sheets. Let rise until double in size. Preheat oven to 450 degrees. Cut diagonal slits on top. Brush with egg-water mixture. Bake 10 minutes; lower temperature to 400 degrees. Bake approximately 20 more minutes or until golden brown and hollow sounding when tapped. Cool on rack.

Breakfast Cheese Pancakes

Yield: 13 pancakes

2 eggs, separated
1/2 cup sour cream
1/2 cup cottage cheese
3/8 cup whole-wheat flour
3/8 teaspoon baking soda
1/4 teaspoon salt
1 1/2 teaspoons sugar
butter
maple syrup

Beat egg whites until stiff; set aside. Beat egg yolks thoroughly; stir in sour cream and cottage cheese. Sift together flour, baking soda, salt and sugar; stir into cheese mixture. Gently fold in egg whites. Drop batter by spoonful onto hot, lightly greased, griddle and cook until bubbly; turn and brown on other side. Serve with butter and warm syrup.

French Toast

Yield: Serves 4

1 day-old French bread or baguette, cut diagonally into thick slices
6 eggs, lightly beaten (or use egg substitute)
2 cups half-and-half
1 tablespoon vanilla extract
1/2 teaspoon ground cinnamon
2 tablespoons light brown sugar
unsalted butter for grilling
confectioner's sugar for dusting
syrup or jam

Arrange bread in single layer in shallow baking dish. Combine eggs, half-and-half, vanilla, cinnamon, and brown sugar. Whisk until blended. Bread should absorb all liquid by pouring mixture over bread; let each side soak 1 to 2 minutes. Preheat griddle; coat generously with butter. When hot, grill bread (do not crowd griddle) until golden and crisp, 3 to 4 minutes per side. Transfer to a warmed platter, sprinkle with confectioner's sugar and serve immediately with your favorite syrup or jam.

Panizikos

2 packages fresh yeast cakes
1/2 cup sugar
1/2 cup oil
1 teaspoon salt
2 eggs, divided
2 cups hot water
7 to 8 cups all-purpose flour
cooking spray
egg wash (remaining egg mixed with 1 teaspoon of water)
sesame seeds, poppy seeds or finely chopped onion

Crumble yeast in large bowl. Add sugar, oil, salt and 1 egg. Mix well with large spoon or with your hands until yeast is dissolved. Add hot water to egg mixture; mix well again. Add 1 cup of flour at a time and mix thoroughly after each cup. Punch and knead dough until easy to handle. Form into a ball. Add a little more flour, if necessary, if dough is still sticky. Coat inside of bowl with cooking spray. Let covered dough rest in bowl for 1 hour. Knead again; rest for another hour. Form into balls the size of a medium lemon, while at the same time working dough. This recipe makes 3 to 4 dozen rolls. May form balls into any shape: knots, twist, etc. Place on greased cookie sheets. Rest for 20 minutes. Brush top of rolls with egg wash. Sprinkle with sesame seeds, poppy seeds or finely chopped onion. Bake at 400 degrees for 12 to 15 minutes or until golden brown.

Apple-Cranberry Pancake

Yield: Serves 6

2 tablespoons butter
1 1/2 cups thinly sliced, peeled apples
1 tablespoon grated orange peel
2 tablespoons fresh lemon juice
2/3 cup whole cranberry sauce
8 eggs, lightly beaten
2 tablespoons flour
1 pinch salt

TOPPING
2 tablespoons each, cinnamon and sugar, mixed
1/2 cup walnut pieces

Preheat oven to 350 degrees. Melt butter in 10-inch ovenproof skillet. Add apples, orange peel, lemon juice and cranberry sauce. Cook over low heat until apples are tender, but not mushy, no more than 5 minutes. Mix remaining ingredients; pour over apples. Stir gently with fork until blended. Sprinkle with topping ingredients. Bake until the eggs are set and topping is browned; approximately 25 to 30 minutes. Serve either hot or at room temperature.

Variation: Can use pears or peaches instead of apples.

Artichoke & Onion Pie

Yield: Serves 12

1/2 cup chopped onions
oil
1 cup mayonnaise
1 8 ounce package cream cheese, room temperature
2 12 ounce cans whole artichokes, chopped
3/4 cup Parmesan cheese
3 cloves garlic, chopped, optional

Preheat oven to 375 degrees. Sauté onions in oil until tender. Mix mayonnaise and cream cheese. Add artichokes, onions and Parmesan cheese. Put into ungreased pie plate. Bake for 15 to 18 minutes.

Variation: Sauté garlic with onion.

Cheese Pie

This recipe can be done in triangle-sized chunks. After you butter the filo and put the filling in, fold in single triangles and place them on an ovenproof dish.

- 1/2 pound feta cheese, either whole or pieces
- 6 eggs
- 1/2 cup chopped parsley
- salt, pepper and nutmeg, to taste
- oil
- 1 package filo pastry sheets
- 4 tablespoons melted butter or margarine

Crush feta to a paste; add eggs, while stirring well. Add parsley, salt, pepper and nutmeg. Spread ovenproof dish with oil; place about 6 to 10 sheets of filo, buttering them on each side. Pour batter and flatten with a spatula. Continue with rest of filo sheets (about 20 to 25 sheets in package). Trim edges with a sharp knife; outline serving squares on top sheet (don't actually cut them; press knife on top surface to mark them in 2-inch squares). Bake at 350 degrees for 30 minutes, or until top sheet is dark brown. Cut squares marked earlier; serve after cooling.

Serbian Cheese Pie

- 6 eggs, beaten
- 1 16 ounce carton small curd cottage cheese
- 1 cup milk
- 1 cup biscuit mix
- 1 pound Jack cheese, diced
- 1/4 pound melted butter, divided

Mix all ingredients together, except butter. Put 1/2 butter in bottom of 9x13 glass ovenproof dish and pour remainder of butter into egg and cheese mixture. Mix well and pour into glass dish. Bake at 350 degrees for 40 to 50 minutes or until golden brown. Let stand a few minutes; cut and serve.

Variation 1: To cut calories use 2% milk and low-fat cottage cheese.

Variation 2: Use a little more biscuit mix and add 1 can drained sweet corn kernels, 2 teaspoons sugar, or fresh sliced mushrooms to mix.

Spinach Pie

CRUST

2 tablespoons butter or margarine
3 cups plus 6 tablespoons flour
1/3 teaspoon salt
1 1/4 teaspoons egg white
1 1/4 teaspoons cream of tartar
1 cup cold water
1 1/2 cups butter or margarine

Work butter or margarine and flour together thoroughly. Make well in center of flour; add salt, egg white and cream of tartar. Mix only until blended. Add cold water, gradually working by hand until sufficient water has been added to make firm, pliant dough. Cover with cloth. Let stand for 12 minutes. Roll out into rectangular shape, 1-inch thick. Divide the dough into 3 parts. Place 1/3 butter or margarine on 1/3 of dough. Fold and roll out. Continue folding, being sure that all of butter or margarine is enclosed. Do the same with the other 2 parts of dough. Refrigerate for 15 minutes. Roll 3/4-inch thick; fold from opposite ends as before. Let stand for 10 minutes. Roll to 1-inch thickness; fold again. Place in refrigerator overnight.

PIE

1 1/2 pounds fresh spinach or 3 10-ounce packages chopped frozen spinach, thawed and drained
1/2 pound feta cheese
1/2 pound Cheddar cheese, grated
3 cups cooked rice
5 eggs, beaten slightly
1 cup chopped onions
2 tablespoons butter

Mix spinach, feta cheese, Cheddar cheese, rice and eggs. Sauté onions in butter. Add to spinach mixture. Divide dough in 2 parts; roll out into 2 rectangles to measure 9x13 inches. In 9x13 pan, place 1 layer of pastry. Cover pastry with spinach-cheese mixture. Cover with 2nd rectangle of dough and pinch edges together. Bake 30 minutes at 350 degrees until golden brown.

Variation 1: 1 1/2 pound package puff pastry may be used instead of making the crust.

Variation 2: If using filo dough, place 1/4 package in bottom of pan, brushing each layer with melted butter. Bake slightly; add spinach mixture. Place remainder of filo dough on top, brushing each layer with melted butter again. Bake 30 minutes at 350 degrees or until golden brown.

Mushroom Quiche

Yield: Serves 6-8

PIE CRUST (can use crust for double crusted pie or single pie crust for quiches)

1 egg
1 tablespoon white vinegar
2 tablespoons sugar
1/2 teaspoon salt
4 1/3 cups flour
1 cup chilled vegetable shortening
3/4 cup butter, somewhat soft but chilled
1/2 cup ice-cold water

Beat egg and vinegar. Sift sugar, salt and flour in medium mixing bowl. Cut chilled shortening into 1/2-inch cubes. Cut in chilled shortening cubes and butter into flour mixture, using a pastry blender, in an up-and-down chopping motion, until mixture resembles coarse crumbs, with some small pea-sized pieces remaining. Sprinkle half of ice-cold water over flour mixture. Using a fork, stir and draw flour from bottom of bowl to top, distributing moisture evenly into flour. Press chunks down to bottom of bowl with fork. Add more water by tablespoon, until dough is moist enough to hold together when pressed together. Test dough for proper moistness by squeezing a marble-sized ball of dough in your hand. If it holds together firmly, do not add any additional water. If dough crumbles, add more water by tablespoonful, until dough is moist enough to form a smooth ball when pressed together. Divide dough in two for double crust or double deep-dish crust, one ball slightly larger than other. Flatten balls into 1/2-inch thick round disks. Wrap dough in plastic wrap. Chill for 30 minutes or up to 2 days. Roll dough (larger ball of dough for double crust pie) from center outward with steady pressure on a lightly floured work surface (or between two sheets of wax or parchment paper) into a circle 2-inches wider than pie plate for bottom crust. Transfer dough to pie plate by loosely rolling around rolling pin. Center rolling pin over pie plate, and then unroll, easing dough into pie plate.

For a single pie crust, trim edges of dough leaving a 3/4-inch overhang. Fold edge under. Flute dough as desired. Bake according to specific recipe directions.

For a double pie crust, roll larger disk for bottom crust, trimming edges of dough even with outer edge of pie plate. Fill unbaked pie crust according to recipe directions. Roll out smaller dough disk. Transfer dough carefully onto filled pie. Trim edges of dough leaving a 3/4-inch overhang. Fold top edge under bottom crust. Press edges together to seal and flute as desired. Cut slits in top crust or prick with fork to vent steam. Bake according to specific recipe directions.

FILLING

3 eggs
2/3 cup whipping cream
1 1/2 teaspoons salt
1/8 teaspoon pepper
1/4 teaspoon nutmeg
1 pound fresh mushrooms, roughly chopped
1/2 cup grated Swiss cheese
2 tablespoons minced shallots
3 tablespoons butter

Beat eggs; blend with whipping cream, salt, pepper and nutmeg. Blend in mushrooms, Swiss cheese and shallots. Pour into pie crust. Dot with butter. Bake at 375 degrees for 1 hour.

Cheese Blintz Cake

BATTER

- 1/2 cup margarine
- 1/4 cup sugar
- 2 eggs, beat one at a time
- 3/4 cup milk
- 1 1/4 cups flour
- 1 teaspoon baking powder
- 1/2 teaspoon salt

FILLING

- 12 ounces cottage cheese
- 8 ounces cream cheese
- 1 egg
- 2 tablespoons instant rice, optional
- 1/4 cup sugar
- 1/4 teaspoon salt

TOPPING

- sour cream
- strawberries, or any fruit

Mix batter ingredients with an electric mixer or hand mixer, until well blended, adding eggs one at a time. Pour half of batter into greased 8-inch square pan. Mix filling ingredients together; spread evenly over batter. Cover with remaining batter; bake at 350 degrees for 30 to 40 minutes. Cut into squares and serve topped with sour cream and strawberries.

Cheese Soufflé

- 6 tablespoons unsalted butter, plus more to butter 6-cup gratin dish
- 6 tablespoons all-purpose flour
- 2 cups cold whole milk
- 1/2 teaspoon freshly ground black pepper
- 5 extra large eggs
- 2 1/2 cups grated Swiss cheese, such as Gruyere
- 3 to 4 tablespoons minced fresh chives

Preheat oven to 400 degrees. Butter 6-cup gratin dish; set aside. Melt butter in saucepan, add flour; mix well with whisk. Cook for 10 seconds; add milk; keep whisking until mixture thickens and comes to a boil. It should be thick and smooth. Remove from heat; stir in salt and pepper. Allow 10 minutes for sauce to cool. Meanwhile, break eggs into bowl; beat well with fork. Add eggs, cheese and chives to sauce; mix well. Pour into gratin dish; bake for 30 to 40 minutes until soufflé is puffy and well browned on top.

Iraqi Fruit and Vegetable Casserole

Yield: Serves 20-30

1 to 2 eggplants, peeled and diced
2 onions, diced
2 green peppers, diced
2 zucchini, diced
2 yams, diced
3 green apples, peeled and diced
1 6 ounce bag dried apricots
1 to 2 cups raisins and currants, mixed together
1 6 ounce bag pitted prunes
dried apples, pine nuts, optional
2 28 ounce cans whole tomatoes
1 to 2 8 ounce cans tomato sauce
2 to 3 cloves garlic, pressed
2 tablespoons chopped dill weed
2 tablespoons chopped basil
salt and pepper, to taste
cayenne pepper, to taste
curry powder, to taste

Place eggplant, onions, green peppers, zucchini and yams in large roasting pan. Add apples, apricots, raisins, currants, prunes, tomatoes and tomato sauce. Add garlic, dill, basil, salt, pepper, cayenne pepper and curry; stir well. Cover; bake at 325 degrees for 2 hours. Taste after 1 hour and adjust seasoning to taste.

Note: This dish should be highly seasoned, but if you're uncertain, put in 2 tablespoons of curry and 1 tablespoon of cayenne pepper at beginning, add more seasoning when you taste it during roasting.

Variation: Can be served hot or cold or with plain yogurt. It's a spectacular dish!

Easy Cheese Soufflé

5 eggs
8 ounces small-curd cottage cheese
8 ounces shredded Cheddar cheese
8 ounces diced green mild chilies
1/4 teaspoon baking powder
avocado, sliced
Roma tomatoes, sliced

Mix all ingredients. Place in 8x10 ovenproof glass dish; top with sliced avocado and Roma tomatoes. Bake 15 minutes at 450 degrees. Lower temperature to 350 degrees and bake 30 minutes longer.

French Toast Soufflé

Yield: Serves 12 slices

10 cups 1-inch cubed sturdy white bread, about 16 one-ounce slices
cooking spray
1 8 ounce block, 1/3-less-fat cream cheese, softened
8 large eggs
1 1/2 cups 2% reduced-fat milk
2/3 cup half-and-half
1 1/4 cups maple syrup, divided
1/2 teaspoon vanilla extract
1/4 cup granulated sugar
1 tablespoon cinnamon
2 tablespoons confectioners sugar

Place bread cubes in 13x9 baking dish, coated with cooking spray. Beat cream cheese at medium-speed of mixer until smooth. Add eggs, 1 at a time, mixing well after each addition. Add milk, half-and-half, 1/2 cup maple syrup, vanilla, sugar and cinnamon; mix until smooth. Pour cream cheese mixture over top of bread, cover and refrigerate overnight. Preheat oven to 375 degrees. Remove bread mixture from refrigerator, let stand on counter for 30 minutes. Bake, uncovered, for 50 minutes or until set. Sprinkle soufflé with confectioners sugar and serve with remaining maple syrup.

Note: A firm white bread produces the best texture in this make-ahead breakfast casserole.

Crispy Black Bean Tacos

Yield: Serves 4

1 15 ounce can low sodium black beans, drained
1/2 teaspoon cumin
1/2 teaspoon salt, optional
4 white or yellow corn tortillas
1 tablespoon lime juice
5 teaspoons (or more) olive oil, divided
2 cups coleslaw mix (or broccoli slaw)
2 green onions, chopped
1/3 cup chopped fresh cilantro
ground black pepper, to taste
hot sauce, to taste
1/3 cup crumbled feta cheese

In a small bowl, combine beans, cumin and salt (if using). Use a fork to partially mash beans; heat in microwave to make beans just warm. Divide mixture between tortillas, spreading it evenly over one side of each. Set aside. In a medium bowl, combine lime juice and 2 teaspoons olive oil. Add coleslaw (or broccoli mix), green onions and cilantro. Toss well. If desired, season with pepper and hot sauce. Set aside. In a large skillet over medium-high heat, heat remaining 3 teaspoons olive oil, or more, if needed. Add tortillas in a single layer, bean side up. Cook in batches, if necessary, for 1 minute. Fold tacos in half, then cook for about another minute per side, or until golden brown. Fill each taco with a quarter of coleslaw or broccoli slaw mixture and feta cheese. If desired, drizzle with additional hot sauce.

Variation: Guacamole may be added in the tortilla or on the side.

Note: Rice accompanies this dish nicely and makes a complete protein with the beans

Spicy Black Bean Cakes with Eggs and Salsa

BLACK BEAN CAKES

4 to 5 Roma tomatoes
1/2 red onion
1 serrano or jalapeño chili
2 teaspoons chopped garlic, divided
2 tablespoons lime juice or 1 lime
salt and pepper, to taste
2 cans black beans
1 tablespoon Sriracha or hot chili sauce
1 cup bread crumbs
canola oil for cooking

Core and halve tomatoes, remove seeds. Small dice tomatoes. Small dice red onion and chili. Mix together with 1 teaspoon garlic and lime juice. Season with salt and pepper. Chill. Drain and rinse black beans. In food processor, add beans, rest of garlic and Sriracha. Pulse a few times to slightly blend beans. Make mixture a little chunky. Using a tablespoon or 1 ounce ice cream scoop, make small balls of black bean mixture. Roll in bread crumbs. With your thumb, gently press down on each ball and form into a small flat cake, silver dollar size. Place on plastic wrap or parchment paper and chill for 2 minutes to set. In sauté pan, heat oil for frying bean cakes. Gently add each cake, sauté until golden brown on both sides. Set aside on paper towel.

POACHED EGGS

8 eggs
1 tablespoon white vinegar
salsa verde or any mild picante sauce
1 avocado, sliced
tomato salsa

In a large saucepan, fill 2/3 with cold water, bring to boil. Add white vinegar. Turn down heat to simmer. Swirl water with a spoon. Break eggs, one at a time, into a cup and pour gently in moving water, cook 3 to 4 minutes; remove with slotted spoon. On each plate, make a puddle of salsa verde or picante sauce. Spread around on plate. Place 2 to 3 bean cakes on each plate. Top with 2 poached eggs, avocado slices and tomato salsa. Serve warm.

Cheese Borekes

Yield: 48 stuffed triangles; serves 15
Prep Time: 1 hour
Cooking Time: 30 minutes

1 egg, lightly beaten
1 bunch fresh parsley, minced
2 cloves garlic, minced
3/4 teaspoon crushed red pepper
6 ounces smoked Gouda cheese, shredded
6 ounces Emmentaler cheese, finely shredded
12 sheets filo dough
3/4 cup unsalted butter, melted

In a medium bowl, whisk together egg, parsley, garlic and crushed red pepper. Mix in Gouda and Emmentaler. One sheet at a time, place filo dough on a flat surface and brush with about 1 tablespoon butter. Cut lengthwise into 4 strips. Place a rounded teaspoon of the egg mixture at one end of each strip. Fold corner of strip over the filling, forming a triangular fold. Continue folding the length of the strip in triangular folds to form a small stuffed triangle. Repeat with remaining filo dough. Preheat oven to 350 degrees. Lightly butter large baking sheet. Arrange stuffed filo triangles in single layer on prepared baking sheet. Bake 30 minutes, or until lightly browned. Serve warm.

Note: The usual filling is feta cheese; this version calls for smoked Gouda and Emmentaler. If you have never worked with filo before, know that it is very fragile and must be kept covered or it will dry out very quickly. This is labor-intensive, but worth it. Divide the filling ahead of time into 48 equal little portions to ensure that all the borekes are uniform in size. This may be made a day before they are baked, and stored covered in refrigerator.

Stay Young Smoothie

Yield: 1 14-ounce smoothie

1/2 cup frozen organic blueberries
1/2 cup frozen organic strawberries
1/2 cup chilled green tea, unsweetened
3/4 cup plain low-fat organic yogurt
2 tablespoons ground flaxseed
2 tablespoons turbinado sugar or other natural sweetener to taste

Combine all ingredients in an electric blender and blend on medium speed until smooth, about 20 seconds. Garnish with fresh berries and serve.

Variation 1: For a nondairy alternative, substitute cultured soy yogurt for dairy yogurt.

Note: Great for breakfast or brunch. For natural sweeteners use apple juice, pineapple juice, honey or artificial sweetener.

Avocado Mousse in Smoked Salmon

10 to 12 slices smoked salmon
1/2 teaspoon grated onion
1 tablespoon lemon juice
1 teaspoon salt
1/2 teaspoon pepper
2 cups mashed avocado
3/4 cup whipping cream
1/2 cup mayonnaise
1 tablespoon kosher gelatin softened in ¼ cup of cold water
1 English cucumber
parsley

Line a 4-cup straight-sided mold with plastic wrap. Overlap 10 to 12 slices of smoked salmon in mold and refrigerate. Add onion, lemon juice and seasonings to avocado. Whip cream until stiff; fold into mayonnaise. Heat gelatin to dissolve and liquefy; add to mayonnaise and cream. Fold into avocado and spoon into salmon lined mold. Refrigerate until set. Turn out onto dish and peel off plastic wrap carefully. Surround with sliced unpeeled English cucumber and decorate with parsley. Bake 15 minutes at 450 degrees. Lower temperature to 350 degrees and bake 30 minutes longer.

Variation: The above can be made in individual molds.

Note: To stop avocado from turning black, immerse into boiling water for a few seconds with skin on.

Roasted Eggplant and Red Pepper Sandwich

1 pound unpeeled eggplant, cut crosswise into rounds
1 roasted or plain onion, sliced
1 loaf focaccia bread, sliced lengthwise
1 clove garlic, optional
1 roasted red bell pepper, sliced
fresh herbs (example: basil)
tomato slices
sliced cheese (your choice)
fat-free salad dressing/Dijon mustard, optional

Spray baking sheet with cooking spray. Lay eggplant slices and onions in single layer. Lightly spray eggplant and onion with cooking spray. Broil 3 inches from heat for 5 minutes; turn eggplant and onion over; broil an additional 5 minutes or until lightly browned. Rub bread with clove of garlic. Arrange eggplant, onion, pepper, herbs, tomato, or whatever your favorite sandwich fixings are, on bread. Place a slice of cheese on top; broil until cheese melts. Drizzle some salad dressing, or spread some Dijon mustard, on top piece of bread.

Note: Use any or all ingredients for sandwich!

Holidays

Holidays

Holidays (continued)

Kashrut

The practice of kashrut in the home allows a Jewish family the opportunity to reconnect with our biblical heritage. The basic dietary laws presented in Leviticus and Deuteronomy represent the disciplines that have been passed from generation to generation and provide us with guidelines, separating meat and milk, as well as permitted and prohibited foods.

Meat and dairy products are never combined in the course of a meal. The use of separate sets of dishes, eating utensils, cooking utensils, pots and pans for both meat and dairy cookery are traditional components of a kosher home. They must also be washed and maintained separately.

Kosher meats consist of cattle, sheep or goat. Kosher animals must chew their cud and have cloven hooves. Fowl considered to be kosher include chicken, ducks, geese, turkey, pigeon and squab. All meat and fowl must be slaughtered according to Jewish Law, which holds fast to the reverence of life, ethics and compassion for the slaughtered animal. Traditionally, kosher butchers were the source of these food items; however, today we can find them in our local supermarkets.

Permitted fish, considered Kosher, have scales and fins. According to the Rabbinical Assembly's Committee on Jewish Law and Standards, swordfish and sturgeon are also kosher. Prohibited are all shellfish such as crab, shrimp, oyster, and lobster.

Neutral or pareve foods, such as fruits, vegetables and eggs, can be consumed with either meat or milk.

Interpretation and variation of the Laws of Kashrut are varied. Sephardic Jews (from Spain, Portugal, Middle East and North Africa) and Ashkenazi Jews (from France, Germany and Eastern Europe) vary somewhat regarding what is permitted and not permitted. For this reason, we suggest that you consult your congregational rabbi for answers regarding specific questions on Kashrut.

Shabbat

The most important day of Jewish week is Shabbat. Each Friday night, we welcome Shabbat with lighting candles and reciting the blessings over wine and challah. Shabbat begins 20 minutes before sundown Friday night, followed by a day of prayer, rest, and renewal.

Blessing over candles:

בָּרוּךְ אַתָּה יְיָ, אֱלֹהֵינוּ מֶלֶךְ הָעוֹלָם, אֲשֶׁר
קִדְּשָׁנוּ בְּמִצְוֹתָיו וְצִוָּנוּ לְהַדְלִיק נֵר שֶׁל שַׁבָּת.

Barukh atah Adonai Eloheinu Melekh ha'olam, asher kid'shanu b'mitzvotav v'tzivanu l'hadlik ner shel Shabbat.

"Blessed are You, LORD, our God, King of the universe, Who has sanctified us with His commandments and commanded us to light the Shabbat candle[s]."

Blessing over wine:

בָּרוּךְ אַתָּה יְיָ, אֱלֹהֵינוּ מֶלֶךְ הָעוֹלָם,
בּוֹרֵא פְּרִי הַגָּפֶן.

Barukh atah Adonai Eloheinu Melekh ha'olam, bo're p'ri ha'gafen.

"Blessed are You, LORD, our God, King of the universe, Who creates the fruit of the vine."

Blessing over challah:

בָּרוּךְ אַתָּה יְיָ, אֱלֹהֵינוּ מֶלֶךְ הָעוֹלָם,
הַמּוֹצִיא לֶחֶם מִן־הָאָרֶץ.

Barukh atah Adonai Eloheinu Melekh ha'olam, ha'motzi lehem min ha aretz.

"Blessed are You, LORD, our God, King of the universe, Who brings forth bread from the earth."

We conclude Shabbat on Saturday night with a Havdallah service. This separates the holiness of Shabbat from the normal weekday.

High Holy Days

Selichot

We begin the High Holy Days with Selichot, reciting prayers of forgiveness, which call upon the individual to look within, reflecting on their actions of the past year. This sets the tone for Rosh Hashanah and Yom Kippur. The Selichot service is held at midnight the Shabbat before Rosh Hashanah; usually the entire community gathers together to attend this service to learn from our rabbis.

Rosh Hashanah

We ask God to inscribe us in the Book of Life.

We bring in the New Year with apples dipped in honey, symbolizing the promise of a sweet year to come. Together we recite the Kiddush (Blessing over wine) and the Shehecheyanu (a prayer of Thanksgiving) as we gather around our holiday table with family and friends.

Sweetness is the theme during these days of celebration: round raisin challahs (to symbolize the crown of the king), tzimmes, kugels and honey cakes.

Blessing for apples and honey:

בָּרוּךְ אַתָּה יְיָ אֱלֹהֵינוּ מֶלֶךְ הָעוֹלָם
בּוֹרֵא פְּרִי הָעֵץ (אָמֵן)

Barukh atah Adonai, Eloheinu, Melekh ha'olam, bo're p'ri ha'etz.

"Blessed are You, LORD, our God, King of the universe, Who creates the fruit of the tree."

Blessing for the New Year:

יְהִי רָצוֹן מִלְּפָנֶיךָ יְיָ אֱלֹהֵינוּ וֵאלֹהֵי אֲבוֹתֵינוּ
שֶׁתְּחַדֵּשׁ עָלֵינוּ שָׁנָה טוֹבָה וּמְתוּקָה

Y'hi ratzon mil'fanekha, Adonai Eloheinu velohei avoteinu, shet'hadesh aleinu shana tova um'tuka.

"May it be Your will, LORD our God and God of our ancestors, that you renew us for a good and sweet year."

Yom Kippur

During the period between Rosh Hashanah and Yom Kippur (ten days of Awe), we take personal inventory of our actions over the past year and prepare ourselves to ask for forgiveness (Al Chait) on Yom Kippur. The period of self-reflection, personal and spiritual atonement and heartfelt prayer for the incoming year culminates with the Day of Atonement. Fasting from food and drink begins from sundown (Kol Nidre) the eve of Yom Kippur, until sundown the next day. During the 25 hours of fasting we reflect on the past year. At this time, we ask God to seal us in the Book of Life. Traditionally, the Fast of Yom Kippur is concluded with the Break Fast, a meal shared with family and friends to celebrate the breaking of the fast and the New Year.

Sukkot and Simchat Torah

Sukkot is a harvest festival, sometimes referred to as the Festival of Booths. It begins five days after Yom Kippur and continues for eight days. The Sukkah that we build symbolizes the temporary shelter built by the Jews as they wandered through the wilderness, once freed from slavery in Egypt. Throughout the holiday we join friends and family to recite the blessings over the lulav and etrog and share a meal in the Sukkah.

Simchat Torah completes the reading of the fifth book of the Torah as well as the start of the Torah reading, beginning with Genesis.

Blessing upon enter a Sukkah:

בָּרוּךְ אַתָּה יְיָ אֱלֹהֵינוּ מֶלֶךְ הָעוֹלָם
אֲשֶׁר קִדְּשָׁנוּ בְּמִצְוֹתָיו וְצִוָּנוּ
לֵישֵׁב בַּסֻּכָּה (אָמֵן)

Barukh atah Adonai Eloheinu Melekh ha'olam, asher kid'shanu b'mitzvotav v'tzivanu leishev ba'sukah.

"Blessed are You, LORD, our God, King of the universe, Who has sanctified us with His commandments and commanded us to dwell in the sukkah."

Hanukkah

The eight nights of Hanukkah commemorate the victory of the Maccabees over the Syrian-Greeks. The miracle stems from the tale of when the Temple was restored and only enough oil was found to last one night, however the light burned for eight nights. Today we light the Hanukiya by lighting one candle each night for the eight nights the oil burned.

Today family and friends gather together to sing songs, play games of dreidel and exchange gifts; celebrating with potato latkes, apple sauce and sufganiot (Israeli jelly donuts).

Shehecheyanu (first night only)

בָּרוּךְ אַתָּה יְיָ, אֱלֹהֵינוּ
מֶלֶךְ הָעוֹלָם, שֶׁהֶחֱיָנוּ, וְקִיְּמָנוּ,
וְהִגִּיעָנוּ לַזְּמַן הַזֶּה.

Barukh atah Adonai Eloheinu Melekh ha'olam, shehecheyanu v'kiy'manu v'higi'anu la z'man ha'ze.

"Blessed are You, LORD, our God, King of the universe, Who has kept us alive, sustained us and enabled us to reach this season."

Blessing for Hanukkah candles:

בָּרוּךְ אַתָּה יְיָ, אֱלֹהֵינוּ מֶלֶךְ הָעוֹלָם,
אֲשֶׁר קִדְּשָׁנוּ בְּמִצְוֹתָיו, וְצִוָּנוּ לְהַדְלִיק
נֵר שֶׁל חֲנֻכָּה.

Barukh atah Adonai Eloheinu Melekh ha'olam, asher kid'shanu b'mitzvotav v'tzivanu l'hadlich ner shel Hanukkah.

"Blessed are You, LORD, our God, King of the universe, Who has sanctified us with His commandments and commanded us to kindle the Hanukkah lights."

Blessing for the miracles of Hanukkah:

בָּרוּךְ אַתָּה יְיָ, אֱלֹהֵינוּ מֶלֶךְ הָעוֹלָם,
שֶׁעָשָׂה נִסִּים לַאֲבוֹתֵינוּ בַּיָּמִים הָהֵם
בַּזְּמַן הַזֶּה.

Barukh atah Adonai Eloheinu Melekh ha'olam, she'asa nisim la'avoteinu ba'yamim ha'heim ba'z'man ha'ze.

"Blessed are You, LORD, our God, King of the universe, Who performed miracles for our ancestors in those days at this time."

Purim

The story of Purim comes from the Book of Esther. As the story is told, shouting, stamping of feet and the noise of the grogger are part of the celebration. Part of the Purim tradition is eating Hamantaschen cookies, costume parades, carnivals and fun for families and friends.

Pesach (Passover)

The Passover Seder symbolizes the exodus of the Jewish people from Egypt, leaving slavery behind in search of the Promised Land. Prior to celebrating Passover, the home is cleaned and every food considered chametz is removed from the home. Detailed instruction regarding kashering the kitchen and permitted foods are made available at your synagogue or online.

This eight-day celebration (seven in Israel) begins with two Seder nights, when we read from the Haggadah about the Jewish people's Exodus from Egypt. The table is set with a seder plate holding the symbols of Passover. Matzah (unleavened bread) is used in place of bread during these eight days to symbolize the haste in which the Jewish people left Egypt. It is on the second night of Passover that we begin to count the Omer (an ancient unit of measurement) for 49 days between Passover and the Feast of Weeks (Shavuot).

Shavuot

Shavuot, or the Feast of Weeks, begins the 50th day after Passover and marks the conclusion of counting the Omer. This springtime holiday commemorates the giving of the Torah to the Israelites at Mount Sinai. Jews eat dairy foods such as blintzes and ice cream.

Easy Bread Machine Challah

LARGE LOAF (1 1/2-2 POUNDS)

1 cup warm water
3 cups bread machine flour
1/4 cup plus 2 tablespoons sugar
3/4 teaspoon salt
3 1/2 tablespoons vegetable or canola oil
3 egg yolks
2 1/4 teaspoons dry active yeast

Makes a large challah. Divide dough in 2 and make 2 medium-size challahs.

MEDIUM LOAF (1 POUND)

2/3 cup warm water
1 3/4 cups plus 2 tablespoons bread machine flour
1/4 cup sugar
1/2 teaspoon salt
2 tablespoons plus 1 teaspoon vegetable or canola oil
2 egg yolks
1 1/2 teaspoons dry active yeast

Makes a medium size challah. Divide dough into 2 and make 2 small Kiddush challahs.

GLAZE

beaten egg whites
water
poppy or sesame seeds

Add dry ingredients in order suggested by your bread machine manual (or follow the above order of ingredients). Yeast will be the last ingredient to be added. Make a little hole in middle of all ingredients, add yeast; cover up little hole. Process ingredients on bread machine's dough cycle. Every bread machine varies (average about 2 1/2 hours). Dough's first rising takes place in bread machine. Lightly spray a cookie sheet with cooking spray. Grease hands with oil. Remove dough from machine; divide into 3 equal parts. If making 2 challahs, divide dough into 2 equal parts, each part into 3 smaller parts. Form each part into a little ball, squeezing out all air bubbles; kneading dough as you go. [At this point, take a pinch of dough; separate it from rest of dough. When ready to bake, put it on cookie sheet with braided challah. This is according to Jewish Law; there is a prayer that goes along with this. This makes bread kosher; this is where expression "challah is taken" comes from.] Place balls on cookie sheet, leaving room to double in size. Cover with a clean kitchen towel and let rise for a minimum of 30 minutes (can be longer) in a warm, but not hot, place. Press dough lightly with your finger, and, if mark remains, dough is ready; if it springs out dough needs to rise longer. This is second rising. On a cutting board, put a small amount of flour; rub some onto hands. Roll each ball of dough in a light dust of flour; make a rope about 12- to 14-inches long. At this point, add raisins or chocolate chips by working them into dough. Braid 3 ropes together, pinching dough together at both ends; tucking ends under. Dough can be made up to 4 days before; can be refrigerated braided or unbraided. Bring to room temperature

Easy Bread Machine Challah (continued)

before baking. Return braid to cookie sheet. Let rise (this is third rising) in warm, but not hot, place for 30 minutes or until double in size. Preheat oven to 350 degrees. Combine egg whites with water. Brush egg whites lightly over the challah. At this point, sprinkle on sesame or poppy seeds or both. Total cooking time is 30 to 40 minutes. After 15 minutes, cover challah with sheet of aluminum foil to keep top from browning too quickly. Check after 30 minutes. Challah should have distinct hollow sound when tapped. Sometimes challah needs a few more minutes. Remove aluminum foil to make sure top is a beautiful golden brown.

Challah #2

Yield: 2 loaves

1/2 cup warm water
2 packages dry yeast

Blend together for 10 minutes or until mixture is bubbly.

ADD

1 1/2 cups water
1/4 cup sugar
1/4 cup oil
1 tablespoon salt
3 eggs
4 cups flour

Mix together until smooth.

KNEADING

3 to 3 1/2 cups flour to be added to dough, as needed

Cover, keep warm, let rise 1 to 2 hours. Cut dough in half. Knead 1 piece on floured surface, until no longer sticky. Take kneaded piece and divide into 2 pieces; 1 piece that is 2/3 of the dough and 1 piece that is 1/3 of the dough. Cut first piece of dough in 3 pieces. Take second piece of dough and cut into 3 pieces. Make 3 ropes from larger pieces and braid. With smaller pieces, make 3 ropes and braid; position on top of larger ropes. Place on lightly greased cookie sheets. Cover with clean cloth, let rise again for about 10 to 20 minutes. If making a second loaf, repeat same directions with the second half of dough or reserve to make at a later time by freezing dough, wrapped in plastic and in aluminum foil.

GLAZE

1 egg yolk
1 teaspoon oil

Beat together; brush on dough. Bake at 425 degrees for 25 to 30 minutes. Remove from oven, place on rack to cool.

Hanukkah Gelt Cookies

COOKIES

1/2 cup margarine or butter
1/2 cup sugar
1/2 cup honey
2 egg yolks
juice and zest of 1 orange
3 1/4 cups flour
1 1/2 teaspoons ginger
1/4 teaspoon salt

ICING

1/2 cup confectioners sugar
1 tablespoon milk
blue food coloring

Cream margarine, sugar and honey until light and fluffy. Blend in egg yolks, juice and zest. Combine flour, ginger and salt. Add margarine mixture to flour. Wrap dough in wax paper and chill several hours (can freeze at this point). Roll dough thin; cut out with Chanukah theme cookie cutters. Bake at 350 degrees for 12 to 15 minutes. Let cool. Mix confectioners sugar, milk and food coloring together. Frost cookies.

Mom's Latkes

6 medium brown potatoes
1 1/2 large onions, shredded and drained
2 eggs, beaten
3 tablespoons flour or matzah meal
1/2 teaspoon black pepper
1 1/2 teaspoons salt
1/2 teaspoon baking powder
oil for frying

Grate potatoes; let stand for 10 minutes and remove liquid. Combined drained potatoes, drained onions, eggs, flour or matzah meal, pepper, salt, baking powder; mix well. In 1 or 2 large skillets heat oil over medium heat. When hot, place large-sized scoop of potato mixture in oil; flattened lightly in form of pancake. When browned, flip until other side is browned. Replace oil between batches. When browned, place latkes on paper towels to soak up extra oil. Keep warm on cookie sheet in 200 to 250 degree oven until ready to serve.

Zucchini Latkes

Yield: 4 dozen 1 1/2-inch latkes

1 pound medium zucchini
1 large thin skinned potato (3/4 pound), unpeeled
1 small onion (4 ounces), peeled
1/2 cup matzo meal
1 large egg, lightly beaten
1 teaspoon fresh lemon juice
1 1/2 teaspoons salt
1/2 teaspoon freshly ground pepper
vegetable oil, for frying

In a food processor, finely grate unpeeled zucchini. Coarsely grate potato and onion. Transfer grated zucchini, potato and onion to a colander; squeeze dry. Let stand for 2 minutes, squeeze again. Transfer vegetable mixture to large bowl. Add matzo meal, egg, lemon juice, salt and pepper; stir to combine. In a large skillet, heat 2 tablespoons of vegetable oil until shimmering. Drop packed spoonfuls of zucchini mixture into skillet; flatten latkes with back of spoon. Cook latkes over moderately high heat until edges are golden, about 1 1/2 minutes; flip and cook until golden on bottom, about 1 minute. Drain on paper towels. Repeat with remaining zucchini mixture, adding more oil to skillet, as needed.

Note: Fried latkes can be kept at room temperature for up to 4 hours. Reheat them on a baking sheet in a 375 degree oven for about 5 minutes, or until warmed through and crisp.

Susan's Purim Rum Balls

Yield: 4 1/2 dozen

1 6 ounce package chocolate bits
1/2 cup sugar
1/4 cup light corn syrup
1/4 cup water
1 1/2 cups vanilla wafer crumbs (5 ounces)
1 cup chopped nuts
1 tablespoon rum
confectioner's sugar

Melt chocolate in double-boiler. Remove from heat; stir in sugar and corn syrup. Blend with water. Add crumbs, nuts and rum. Form in balls; roll in confectioner's sugar.

Hamentashen

DOUGH

2/3 cup butter or margarine
1 cup sugar
3 eggs
2 tablespoons honey, melted
2 tablespoons orange juice or water
salt
2 cups flour (plus approximately 1 1/2 to 2 cups flour)
1 tablespoon baking powder

Cream butter or margarine and sugar together. Add eggs, beating well after each egg. Add honey, juice or water and dash of salt. Slowly mix in 2 cups flour and baking powder. Add rest of flour slowly, about a cup at a time, until you have a soft dough. Put onto a floured board and continue to add flour until dough is manageable. Dough can be refrigerated overnight, or at least for 2 hours, until firm enough to roll out. Divide dough into 3 parts, flatten with hand, roll gently and cut-out in circles using 2 1/2- to 3-inch cookie cutters.

FILLING

pitted prunes
raisins
several dried apricots
nuts
lemon juice
apricots jam

GLAZE

1 egg, beaten

Preheat oven to 375 degrees. Grind together prunes, raisins and apricots. Add chopped nuts, lemon juice and jam. Mix together well. Place 1 teaspoon of filling in center of each cookie circle. Pinch one side up. Turn and pinch second and third sides to make a triangular shape. Leave a little bit of filling showing at the top. Place cookies on parchment paper on cookie sheet, brush with beaten egg for sheen; bake until nicely browned, 10 to 15 minutes.

Variation: Another filling is 1 can poppy seed mix, chopped nuts and jam. Mix together well.

Note: Recipe can be doubled or tripled.

Farfel

1 large onion, chopped
vegetable oil
1 box farfel
3 cups boiling water
salt and pepper, to taste

Fry onion in oil until golden. Add farfel; pour boiling water over farfel. Add salt and pepper. Cover farfel; simmer 8 to 10 minutes. Cook until water boils away. Bake in 350 degree oven for 20 minutes; serve.

Kishka Casserole for Passover

Yield: Serves 8-10
Prep Time: 15 minutes

1/2 cup grated Cheddar cheese
1/2 cup chopped celery
3 cups crushed egg matzos
1 cup margarine, melted
1 large onion, chopped
4 cloves garlic, minced
2 eggs, beaten
salt, to taste
1/4 teaspoon pepper
1/4 teaspoon poultry seasoning

Preheat oven to 350 degrees. In bowl, combine all ingredients and mix well. Place a 20-inch piece of aluminum foil on baking sheet. Spray aluminum foil with cooking spray. Place mixture on aluminum foil and shape into a 16-inch roll. Bring up sides of aluminum foil (allowing room for expansion). Fold short sides up; roll over, seam side down. Bake on baking sheet for 45 minutes. Let cool. Slice in 1/2-inch slices.

Megina

This layered casserole consists of a savory meat filling between 2 layers of egg-softened matzah.

2 pounds lean ground beef or turkey
1 large onion, diced
2 tablespoons vegetable oil
1 teaspoon salt
1/4 teaspoon pepper
1/2 cup chopped fresh parsley
8 eggs, beaten, divided
6 matzahs, divided

Preheat oven to 350 degrees. In large skillet, brown meat and onion in oil. Add salt, pepper and parsley. Cook 1 additional minute. Remove from heat. Add 4 beaten eggs to meat mixture; blend well. Set aside. Grease 9x13x3 pan. Soak 3 matzahs (1 at a time) in warm water, until just softened. Don't let them fall apart! Soak softened matzahs in 2 beaten eggs, until eggs are absorbed. Line bottom of pan with matzahs. Spoon meat mixture over matzahs, spreading evenly. Soak remaining 3 matzahs in warm water until soft, then dip in 2 remaining beaten eggs until absorbed. Place over meat filling. Bake 45 minutes. Serve hot.

Zucchini Quashado

4 cups shredded unpeeled zucchini
1 cup small-curd cottage cheese
1/2 cup crumbled feta cheese
4 eggs, well beaten
1/2 teaspoon salt
1 cup farfel or crumbled matzah
2 tablespoons vegetable oil
1/2 cup grated Parmesan cheese or more to your taste

Mix first 6 ingredients thoroughly. Add oil to a 13x9 baking pan. Pour zucchini mixture into pan. Spread Parmesan cheese evenly on top. Bake at 400 degrees for 45 minutes to 1 hour. Best when served warm..

Individual Passover Spinach Soufflé

Prep Time: 20 minutes

1/4 cup chopped green pepper
1 cup chopped onion
1/2 cup chopped celery
1 1/2 cups grated raw carrot
6 tablespoons margarine
1 10 ounce package frozen chopped spinach
3 eggs, beaten
1 1/2 teaspoons salt
1/4 teaspoon pepper
3/4 cup matzah meal

Saute green pepper, onion, celery and carrot in margarine for about 10 minutes, stirring occasionally. Cook spinach; drain. Combine vegetables. Add eggs, salt, pepper and matzah meal. Spoon into 12 greased muffin tins. Bake at 350 degrees for 45 minutes. Allow to cool for 10 minutes. Remove from pan.

Passover Stuffing

3 to 4 tablespoons oil
2 large onions, chopped
1 1/2 cups chopped mushrooms
1 cup chopped celery
1 box matzah farfel or 1 pound matzah broken and crumbled
2 14 ounce cans undiluted kosher chicken soup or 3 cups prepared soup
1 egg, beaten
1/4 teaspoon pepper
1 teaspoon salt
3/4 tablespoon paprika
1 tablespoon parsley

Heat oil in an electric frying pan. Add onions and cook until translucent. Add mushrooms and celery. Cook about 5 minutes longer. Stir mixture, so that vegetables do not stick. Add more oil, if necessary. Add matzah farfel or broken matzah to vegetables and toast slightly. Mix together soup, egg, pepper, salt, paprika and parsley. Add to vegetable and matzah mixture. Cover and cook about 5 to 7 minutes adding water or soup if necessary. Let cool. May be used to stuff turkey or Cornish hens or can be baked to serve as a side dish.

Squash Kugel

2 pounds zucchini, grated with food processor, drained
1 onion, grated
1 large Idaho potato, grated, drained
6 eggs, beaten
1/2 cup matzah meal
1/4 pound margarine, melted
salt and pepper, to taste
1 teaspoon MSG food enhancer, optional

Combine zucchini, onion, potato, eggs, matzah meal, margarine, salt, pepper and MSG food enhancer. Bake in 13x9 greased casserole dish for 50 minutes at 350 degrees.

Carrot Tzimmes Kugel

1 cup grated sweet potato (medium size)
1 cup grated carrot
1 cup peeled and grated apple
1/2 cup raisins
1/2 cup chopped prunes
1/2 cup sugar
1/2 cup matzah meal
2 tablespoons lemon juice
1/2 teaspoon cinnamon
1/2 teaspoon salt
1/2 cup margarine or oil

Mix all ingredients together in a large bowl. Pour into greased soufflé or baking dish. Bake at 350 degrees for 45 minutes or until light brown.

Note: Double the recipe for Passover; grate everything in a food processor.

Matzah Tostada Yucatan Style

ACHIOTE SMOKED SEA BASS

1/4 cup rice vinegar
1/4 cup orange juice
1/4 cup olive oil
1/2 pound smoked sea bass or any smoked white fish, sliced
salt, to taste

In a bowl, mix rice vinegar and orange juice. Emulsify olive oil by whisking it into vinegar mixture. Toss liquids with smoked fish and season well with salt. Place fish mixture in refrigerator for 2 hours.

CRISPY MATZAH TORTILLAS

2 cups matzah cake meal
1 teaspoon salt
1 cup warm water
1 tablespoon olive oil, plus additional for frying

Mix in a bowl by hand: matzah cake meal, salt, warm water and olive oil. With hands, form 1 1/2 inch balls, then roll between plastic wrap to form tortilla shape. Using 2 tablespoons olive oil, preheat nonstick griddle or pan on medium flame. Place matzah tortilla on griddle. Cook on both sides, until nice and soft. Pour additional olive oil into a frying pan. Preheat oil to 300 degrees. Fry tortillas in oil until crisp.

HORSERADISH-JALAPEÑO SALSA

1/2 small red onion, diced
2 tablespoons grated fresh horseradish
1 small seedless jalapeño, chopped
2 tablespoons lemon juice
2 tablespoons orange juice
1/2 tablespoon honey
salt, to taste

Mix onion, horseradish, jalapeño, lemon juice and orange juice with honey. Season well with salt. Serve smoked fish with matzah tortillas, topped with salsa.

Variation: Add mango and avocado for garnish.

Cholesterol-Free Matzah Balls

Yield: Makes 20-24 matzah balls

1 cup matzah meal
1 teaspoon salt
1 carton egg substitute
4 tablespoons margarine (1/2 stick) melted and cooled
4 tablespoons cold water
instant chicken bouillon

Combine matzah meal, salt and egg substitute; mix well. Add margarine and water; stir into batter. Cover bowl and refrigerate several hours or overnight. Wet hands in cold water and shape mixture into walnut-size balls. Drop into gently boiling water flavored with instant chicken bouillon. Reduce heat; cover and cook 30 to 40 minutes. Transfer matzah balls with a slotted spoon to heated chicken soup.

Sephardic Haroset

6 ounces dried dates, pitted
6 ounces figs
6 ounces apricots
6 ounces prunes, pitted
3 ounces raisins
4 apples, peeled, cored and sliced
1/2 cup or to taste slivered almonds, no skin
blackberry wine or other sweet Passover wine to taste
1 tablespoon cinnamon or to taste
1 teaspoon Allspice or to taste
1 teaspoon ginger or to taste
1/2 teaspoon cloves or to taste

Pulse all ingredients, except wine and seasonings, in food processor. Mix in wine and seasonings. Refrigerate overnight. Flavors will meld together. May need to add seasoning or wine the next day. Good on matzah. Refrigerate to store.

Passover Meringue Kisses

Yield: 45 meringue kisses
Prep Time: 20 minutes

2/3 cup egg whites
2 2/3 cups confectioner's sugar
3/4 cup chopped walnuts
matzah cake meal

Combine egg whites and sugar in top of double boiler. Put over hot, not boiling, water and beat mixture with a mixer, vigorously, until stiff peaks form. Carefully fold in walnuts. Drop teaspoons of mixture onto buttered baking pan which has been sprinkled with matzah cake meal. Bake at 300 degrees for 25 minutes.

Margie's Passover Macaroons

8 egg whites
3 teaspoons vanilla
1 1/3 cups granulated sugar
1/2 cup cake meal (or flour if not for Passover)
6 cups shredded coconut (approximately 2 bags)
2 cups chocolate chips
vegetable oil

Beat egg whites until frothy or almost in peaks. Mix vanilla, sugar, cake meal and coconut into egg whites. Spoon onto greased cookie sheet. Bake at 325 degrees for 15 minutes or until golden brown. Cool completely on rack. Melt 2 cups chocolate chips with 2 capfuls of vegetable oil in microwave. Stir. Dip edge of cookies in mixture and put on wax paper-covered cookie sheet to cool. Refrigerate to set chocolate. Keep in refrigerator until ready to use.

Passover Date Puffs

Yield: 26 puffs

2 eggs whites
1 cup confectioners sugar
1 cup finely chopped pecans
1 cup finely chopped dates
1/2 cup shredded coconut

Beat egg whites until stiff and dry. Gradually add sugar; beat until very stiff. Fold in pecans, dates and coconuts with spatula. Drop teaspoons of mixture onto greased baking pan. Bake at 250 degrees for 20 minutes.

Variation: Can be dipped in melted chocolate or add chocolate chips.

Passover Brownies

2 sticks margarine or butter, room temperature
3 cups sugar
6 eggs
6 tablespoons potato starch
6 tablespoons matzah cake meal
1 teaspoon vanilla
1 scant cup cocoa
chopped nuts, optional
confectioners sugar

Preheat oven to 350 degrees. Cream the margarine and sugar. Add eggs; beat well. Add potato starch and matzah cake meal, beating well. Mix cocoa with enough water to make a paste or icing consistency. Add this and vanilla (nuts if desired) to batter. Mix well. Grease a 9x13 pan; pour batter into pan. Bake for 30 minutes. DO NOT OVERBAKE. Cut immediately into small squares when brownies are cool. Sprinkle with confectioners sugar on top.

Variation: Add 1 cup chocolate chips to make brownies richer.

Chaiky's Passover Brownies

Yield: Makes 25 1 1/4-inch squares

1/2 cup oil
1 cup sugar
3 eggs
1/2 cup matzah cake meal
1/3 cup cocoa
1/2 cup chopped nuts, optional

Mix oil and sugar. Add eggs and mix again. Sift matzah cake meal and cocoa together; add to mixture. Add nuts; mix thoroughly. Pour batter into greased 8-inch square pan. Bake at 350 degrees for 25 minutes. Cut into squares while still warm.

Fruit Casserole

Yield: Serves 10

1 can apricot halves
1 can peach halves
1 can pitted dark cherries
1 can tropical fruit salad
1 can pitted plums
1 23 ounce jar chunk applesauce

Drain everything but applesauce. Put into a deep casserole dish, uncovered. Bake at 325 degrees for 3 hours. Recipe can be doubled or tripled, baking time is the same.

Note 1: Because casserole can bubble over, it can be placed on a rimmed baking sheet.

Note 2: Serve with whipped cream, thawed nondairy whipped topping or vanilla ice cream.

Matzah Toffee

matzah
1 cup butter
1 cup sugar
1 tablespoon vanilla
2 1/2 cups chocolate chips
chopped nuts, optional
shredded coconut, optional

Preheat oven to 350 degrees. Line cookie sheet with aluminum foil. Line cookie sheet with a single layer of matzah. Melt butter with sugar over low/medium heat. Simmer until sugar is completely dissolved into butter, at least 2 minutes. Stir constantly. As mixture simmers, add vanilla. Pour butter/sugar mixture over matzah. Spread as evenly as possible. Bake for 10 minutes. As soon as matzah comes out of oven, spread chocolate chips over hot matzah, as evenly as possible. If chips do not melt completely, return cookie sheet to turned-off oven, until chocolate chips melt. Cool overnight in refrigerator. Peel matzo off foil and break into pieces.

Variation: Sprinkle chopped nuts and/or shredded coconut on top of melted chocolate.

Strawberry Apple Macaroon Crumble

Yield: Serves 10-12

7 ounces almond paste, crumbled
1 cup plus 1 tablespoon sugar
2 large egg whites
1/2 cup matzah cake meal
1/4 teaspoon salt
3 pounds tart apples, peeled, cored and sliced
1 pound strawberries, rinsed, hulled and sliced
2 tablespoons lemon juice
1 1/2 tablespoons potato starch

In a food processor, blend almond paste and 1 cup sugar. Add egg whites, matzah cake meal and salt. Blend until well-incorporated (should resemble wet cookie dough). In large bowl, mix apples, strawberries, lemon juice, potato starch and 1 tablespoon sugar. Spread fruit mixture in a 2 1/2- to 3-quart baking dish. Pat almond mixture over fruit. Bake in 350 degree oven, until topping is browned and fruit bubbles (about 40 to 45 minutes). Let stand at least 10 minutes.

Matzah Charlotte

4 matzahs
9 eggs
1 cup sugar
1 tablespoon cinnamon
2 apples, peeled, cored and grated
1 1/2 cups yellow raisins
2/3 cup blanched slivered almonds
rind of 1 lemon
1/4 cup oil

Preheat oven to 375 degrees. Break matzahs into pieces; soak in cold water. Beat eggs, sugar and cinnamon until light. Stir in apples, raisins, almonds and lemon rind. Squeeze water out of matzahs; add to egg mixture. Oil a 9x13 ovenproof baking dish. Pour mixture into pan. Bake for 45 minutes.

Passover Sponge Cake

Prep Time: 30 minutes

8 extra-large eggs
1 1/2 cups sugar
3/4 cup potato flour
1/4 cup matzah cake meal
1 lemon rind
juice of 1 lemon

Separate eggs. Beat egg whites and gradually add sugar, 1 tablespoon at a time, until very stiff. Sift potato flour and matzah cake meal together. Fold dry ingredients into egg whites, 1/3 cup at a time. Beat egg yolks; add lemon rind and juice. Fold into mixture. Pour into a dry 10-inch tube pan. Bake for 1 hour at 350 degrees. Cool for 1 hour then cut around edges to loosen.

Passover Blueberry Muffins

Yield: Makes 12 muffins

1 cup sugar
1/2 cup margarine
3 eggs
1/4 cup potato starch
1/2 cup cake meal
1/4 teaspoon salt
1 cup frozen blueberries, slightly thawed

Preheat oven to 350 degrees. Combine sugar and margarine. Add eggs, one at a time. Mix in dry ingredients. Stir in blueberries gently. Fill lined muffin tins, bake for 45 minutes. Can be frozen.

Flourless Chocolate Cake

1 stick unsalted butter plus extra butter for buttering wax paper
4 ounces fine quality bittersweet chocolate
3/4 cup sugar
3 large eggs
1/2 cup unsweetened cocoa powder

Preheat oven to 375 degrees. Line bottom of an 8-inch round baking pan with wax paper; butter wax paper. Chop chocolate into small pieces. In a double boiler, melt chocolate with butter, stirring until smooth. Remove from heat and whisk in sugar. Add eggs 1 at a time, mixing well after each egg. Sift cocoa powder over chocolate mixture and whisk until just combined. Pour batter into pan and bake for 25 minutes or until top forms a thin crust. Cool cake in pan for 5 minutes, then transfer to serving plate and dust with more cocoa powder.

Variation: Can also be dusted with confectioners sugar.

Passover Lemon Meringue Pie

Yield: Serves 10

CRUST

1 1/2 cans coconut macaroons
1 egg white

Put macaroons into food processor and pulse until chopped. Mold macaroons into pie plate and glaze with beaten egg white. Bake at 350 degrees for 10 minutes.

FILLING

4 large egg yolks
3 large eggs
1/2 cup sugar
3/4 cup fresh lemon juice
2 tablespoons potato starch
1 stick chilled butter, cut into small pieces

In top of double boiler, whisk together egg yolks, eggs, sugar, lemon juice and potato starch. Cook over medium heat, stirring constantly until thick enough to coat spoon. Do not let mixture boil. Remove mixture from heat and stir in butter. Pour into crust.

MERINGUE

4 large egg whites
1/4 teaspoon potato starch
1/4 teaspoon cream of tartar
1/4 cup sugar
1 teaspoon vanilla

Beat egg whites at medium speed until foamy. Beat in potato starch and cream of tartar, until soft peaks form. Gradually beat in sugar and vanilla at high speed, until stiff (but not dry) peaks form. Spoon meringue into large pastry bag fitted with star tip. Pipe meringue decoratively over filling to edge of crust. Bake pie at 350 degrees, until meringue is golden, 12 to 15 minutes.

Potato Muffins

2 eggs
2 cups water
1/2 cup oil
1 6 ounce box potato pancake mix
1/4 cup matzah meal

Beat eggs; add water, oil and mix. Add potato pancake mix and matzah meal. Let mixture stand for 5 minutes or more. Grease muffin tins with cooking spray. Fill muffin tins and bake at 350 degrees for 1 hour.

Note: You can prepare these earlier in the day and re-bake them, until golden brown, before serving. These freeze well and can be used for Passover or during the year.

Helpful Hints for Dairy Substitutions

Ingredient	Substitution
1 cup skim milk	1/3 cup instant nonfat dry milk plus 3/4 cup water
	4 tablespoons powdered whole milk plus 7/8 cup water
	4 tablespoons powdered nonfat dry milk and 2 tablespoons melted fat (butter or margarine) plus 1 cup water
	1/2 cup pareve milk plus 1/2 cup water
	1 cup fruit juice or 1 cup potato water (for baking)
	7/8 cup liquid skim milk plus 3 tablespoons melted butter (for cooking only)
1 cup whole milk	1/4 cup pareve milk plus 3/4 cup water
	1/2 cup evaporated milk plus 1/2 cup water
1 cup light cream	1 cup undiluted evaporated milk
1 cup heavy cream	3/4 cup milk plus 1/3 cup melted butter (for cooking only, not whipping)
1 cup sour milk or buttermilk (for baking)	1 tablespoon lemon juice or 1 tablespoon vinegar plus enough milk to measure 1 cup (allow to stand 5 minutes)
1 cup buttermilk	1 cup yogurt

Helpful Hints for Meat Substitutions and Non-Kosher Meats and Fish

ground meat	textured soy granules
chunks of meat	soy chunks
bacon	kosher beef fry or bacon flavored soy chips
smoked meats	pastrami, salami or smoked veal shoulder
shrimp	flounder fillets*
scallops	halibut, haddock or cod chunks*
crabmeat salad	halibut or sole*
lobster	haddock or halibut*

*The substitute fish is cut into bite-size pieces, either chunks or strips of varying lengths, and prepared to simulate the appearance of the fish being substituted. Tip: semi-frozen or chilled fish can be cut into cubes more easily.

Helpful Hints for Vegetable Measurement Conversions

4 cups sliced raw potatoes	4 medium-sized potatoes
4 cups diced raw potatoes	4 medium-sized potatoes
3 cups mashed potatoes	1 1/2 potatoes, raw, unpeeled or 2 cups instant potato buds
3 cups sliced sweet potatoes or yams	3 medium-sized sweet potatoes or yams
4 cups cooked cut green beans	1 pound fresh green beans
1 cup shelled peas	1 pound fresh peas
1 cup chopped onion	1 large onion
4 cups shredded cabbage	1 pound head cabbage
2 1/2 cups canned tomatoes	1 pound can tomatoes
5 medium carrots	1/2 pound carrots
1 cup grated raw carrots	1 large carrot
2 cups diced carrots	3 to 4 medium-sized carrots
2 cups diced beets	4 medium-sized beets

Helpful Hints for Seasoning Substitutions

1 teaspoon dry mustard	1 tablespoon prepared mustard
1 cup ketchup or chili sauce	1 cup tomato sauce, 1/4 cup sugar, 2 tablespoons vinegar, 1/4 teaspoon ground cloves (for cooking)
1 teaspoon Italian seasoning	1/4 teaspoon each of basil, oregano, thyme, rosemary, sage and a dash of cayenne
1/2 pound mushrooms	1 1/2 ounces dried mushrooms, reconstituted
1 teaspoon allspice	1/2 teaspoon cinnamon, 1/8 teaspoon ground cloves
1 average sized lemon, juice	2 tablespoons bottled lemon juice
1 small onion, chopped	1 tablespoon instant minced onion, rehydrated, or 1/4 cup frozen chopped onion
1 clove garlic	1/4 teaspoon garlic powder
1 tablespoon chopped fresh herbs	1 teaspoon crushed dry herbs
1/4 cup soy sauce	3 tablespoons Worcestershire sauce plus 1 tablespoon water

Valley Beth Shalom Sisterhood

Deliciously Kosher

15739 Ventura Blvd.

Encino, CA 91436

Visit www.deliciouslykosher.com to place orders online

Please send me __________ copies

of **Deliciously Kosher** at	$29.99	$____________
Postage and Handling (First copy)	$6.00	$____________
Additional copies to same address	$4.00	$____________
California Residents, please add appropriate sales tax (Los Angeles - 9.0%)		$____________
	TOTAL	$____________

Please make checks payable to VBS Sisterhood ☐ Check Enclosed

Please charge my ☐ VISA ☐ Mastercard ☐ Gift Wrap ($4.00 per book) ☐ Gift Card ($1.00 per book)

Card Account # ☐☐☐☐☐☐☐☐☐☐☐☐☐☐☐☐

Expiration Date: Month ☐☐ Year ☐☐ CVV# ☐☐☐

Card Holder's Signature ____

(Complete reverse side of order form)

— — — — — — — — — — — — — — — — — — — —

Valley Beth Shalom Sisterhood

Deliciously Kosher

15739 Ventura Blvd.

Encino, CA 91436

Visit www.deliciouslykosher.com to place orders online

Please send me __________ copies

of **Deliciously Kosher** at	$29.99	$____________
Postage and Handling (First copy)	$6.00	$____________
Additional copies to same address	$4.00	$____________
California Residents, please add appropriate sales tax (Los Angeles - 9.0%)		$____________
	TOTAL	$____________

Please make checks payable to VBS Sisterhood ☐ Check Enclosed

Please charge my ☐ VISA ☐ Mastercard ☐ Gift Wrap ($4.00 per book) ☐ Gift Card ($1.00 per book)

Card Account # ☐☐☐☐☐☐☐☐☐☐☐☐☐☐☐☐

Expiration Date: Month ☐☐ Year ☐☐ CVV# ☐☐☐

Card Holder's Signature ____

(Complete reverse side of order form)

Share Jewish Heritage with friends and family by sending a copy of **Deliciously Kosher**

Mail book to: Name ______________________________

Address ______________________________

City ______________________________

State ______________________ Zip Code ______________

All copies will be sent to your address unless otherwise specified. If you wish books sent as gifts, please note below and enclose your gift cards with this order. If you would like a brief message inscribed in the front of the book send message(s) on a separate piece of paper.

Send gift(s) to:	Addresses(es)

Share Jewish Heritage with friends and family by sending a copy of **Deliciously Kosher**

Mail book to: Name ______________________________

Address ______________________________

City ______________________________

State ______________________ Zip Code ______________

All copies will be sent to your address unless otherwise specified. If you wish books sent as gifts, please note below and enclose your gift cards with this order. If you would like a brief message inscribed in the front of the book send message(s) on a separate piece of paper.

Send gift(s) to:	Addresses(es)